T0208216

WHO IS YOUR BROTHER IN 1ST JOHN?

Samual Hadley

WESTBOW
P R E S S®
A DIVISION OF THOMAS NELSON
& ZONDERVAN

WestBow Press books may be ordered through booksellers or by contacting:

WestBow Press
A Division of Thomas Nelson & Zondervan
1663 Liberty Drive
Bloomington, IN 47403
www.westbowpress.com
1 (866) 928-1240

ISBN: 978-1-9736-5908-2 (sc)
ISBN: 978-1-9736-5910-5 (hc)
ISBN: 978-1-9736-5909-9 (e)

Library of Congress Control Number: 2019904058

Print information available on the last page.

WestBow Press rev. date: 4/8/2019

PREFACE

In simple words, 1st John says, "He who says he is in the light and hates his brother is in darkness, but he that loves his brother has no cause for stumbling, but he that hates his brother is in darkness and does not know where he is going." My question is this. In reference to your brother, who is John writing about? Hate or love who? I know that you think you know, but I promise by the end of this book, you will know that you are wrong. There is no way for you to know who your brother is except to read this book. Grab a highlighter and mark the places where you disagree with the logic as you read, so that at the end of the book you can come back and see how many times you changed your mind. Your about to step into a non-fiction Biblical mystery that will change your mind on your "brother" and is an amazing eye opener to the Christian that believes in the Word of God. It's not a secret message, it's the main message and only message of 1st John and it's from the Bible.

Jesus said, "He that hath ears to hear, let him hear". Mark 4:9 King James Bible

1

YOU DON'T KNOW

Before being tossed at sea till the ship finally failed, he had promised by the Word of God all would make it to the shore of Malta, and now that all are accounted for and safely ashore, he can finally sit by the fire and warm himself. As he reaches to put some sticks on the fire, a poisonous viper strikes and latches onto his hand. In disgust, he grabs the snake and throws it in the fire. The apostle then pulls up a cozy seat by the fire, and with a smirk of a chuckle, he thinks, I almost forgot about that. Luke sees his smirk and has to look away to keep from laughing like a hysterical lunatic.

You can spend your whole life studying the Holy Bible; going to school, getting a degree, teaching, preaching and pressing in like no other, and still not know the answer to this question. Who is your brother in 1st John? The fact is, there is no way for you to know. What do I mean? In the study of the Word, we use all sources available to assist in our understanding of what the Word actually means. We rely on scholars and commentators and historians and the founding fathers for our guidance. We dissect the Word with dictionary, lexicon and period-correct concordance. We use well prepared study guides. Then we cross-reference these materials with the Word and compare our translation with our preferred religion. What we come up with we call biblical truth.

Thus, I will ask right here. Do you believe that the Holy Bible is the true word of God? Most Christians say, "I believe the Holy Bible to be the true living word of God." Some churches, to fit their agenda say, "I believe the Holy Bible to be the true word of God, as long as it is translated correctly." And that means certain words mean certain things to benefit their religion. So, I ask again. Do you believe the Holy Bible is translated correctly, and is the true word of God? I do!

The truths I expose in this book will in no way change who Jesus is. They will only glorify Him. It will not change biblical truth. It will simplify biblical truth. But, having this new understanding of the Word can affect your religion. The purpose in my writing is not to harm religion, but rather to enhance it. However, I cannot worry about that aspect and proclaim truth. From my point of view, I do not see one religious institution that gets it one hundred percent right. Some are closer than others. But with that said, to this very day, I have never met a church leader who was not doing, but what the Lord has called him to do. And I have not met a church leader to this very day that has a clue as to the answer of this question. Who is your brother in 1ˢᵗ John? At some point, as you flip the following pages, if you are a church leader, you will start having to retranslate the Bible, or step away for religious reasons, or just pretend that I am a fool. To see what I show may require prayer, or maybe, I just might be crazy and what I'm showing is not really there. But once we get to the Word, my foundation will be only the Word. And when using only the Word, the answer to this question becomes an easy one. So, who is your brother? Take a guess.

A couple years ago, my wife and I were getting ready for a study on 1ˢᵗ John, so we read the letter twice and discussed its message thoroughly to where we were both comfortable as to its meaning. But later, while driving and contemplating the letter further on my own, I found one line to seem out of place. If you read any works from the commentators or scholars on many of the books of the New Testament, there is often a statement saying, "scholars believe", or "some scholars believe", and then they alter the book in some way. I will use the Gospel of Mark as an example. "Some scholars believe the last versus of Mark were added at a later date". I believed I had just found one of those out of place lines. So I prayed, Lord Jesus, is this line supposed to be in the book of 1st John? Instantly, my eyes were opened.

We are taught that the Holy Bible is true and woven together by a single thread. That thread is Jesus Christ. Only we treat the book and teach the book, as though that thread is no more than a binder to hold the books together. Where in truth, that thread knots every word to each other in a way that no other novel has been able to match. Yet, because of presuppositions as to what our religions say, we cannot see the actual story in front of us. The New Testament was written in Greek and translated to English via a long path, but none the less, it's just that simple plus time. When the first-century Christians were reading these letters, there is no doubt they understood what they meant. And by the time the books were canonized some understanding was already aloof. In the translations and wisdoms of everything, some meaning got lost. Like for instance, in 1st John who is your brother?

In the Gospels, Jesus said over and over, beware of the Pharisees, Sadducees and the Scribes. And what did they represent? They represented the religion of God. They represented the old covenant. And why did Jesus speak in parables? To confound the wise, while edifying his followers, right. And who was He confounding, these wise? That would be the Pharisees, Sadducees and the Scribes. Those on the wayside, that wanted to kill Him. The group that studied the Word of God for a living. They were the representatives of God, and when Jesus spoke, it was meant as confusion to them.

And now two thousand years later, we have the evidence of the New Testament, written by the followers of Jesus, at the time of His life and death, and they all confirm His resurrection from the dead. And we have Paul, who was a Pharisee, transformed and confirming that Jesus, indeed, rose from the dead. So, my point being, as Christians, from these New Testament books we obtain our knowledge in this belief, that Jesus died for our sins, and rose from the grave, and ascended to heaven, and is the Son of God. And if we repent of our sins, and believe in Him, we will join Him in heaven. I hope that fits all Christian belief.

How is it, that a biblically unschooled, uneducated truck driver has New Testament questions with answers that the Christian world cannot see? If you are clergy, don't be offended, oh, but you will be. The word of God has a way of confusing the wise. As for me, well the Lord loves working through the weak and least capable. Also, God plus one is a majority. When you finish this book, you will likely join us and the majority will grow. In the Gospel of John, Nicodemus, a Pharisee, met Jesus one night, because he knew that He was of God, and Nicodemus got it. It was not his job to interfere, but he honored Jesus burial with incense, why? Because Jesus is God. Duh. Myself, I will sit under the broom tree, because my heart is not for the masses but for truth. Thus, when you read this little book, and you get it, and it's your calling, well, get on your knees. Amen. Then jump.

As I said, I believe the Holy Bible to be the Word of God. My favorite is the New King James Version, but for copywrite reasons, as I write and reference, I will be using the King James Version. I will be referring and talking about other study Bibles for their intellectual content only. But as for the actual Word, I will be using the KJV. The Word of God in the New Testament is a translation from Greek to modern times and I usually have no problem with other translations, it's just that I find it as part of the understanding problem, especially in 1ˢᵗ John. They all tell the same story right. That's really good. We cross reference each word, and study each word in each version, and focus on the value of each word, and we miss the story. That's really bad. The newer translations of the Word, in the attempt to simplify and modernize the writing, have changed words from the Greek that change the overall story. In 1ˢᵗ John 5:1 the word *him* is used three times in one sentence in the NKJV and all older versions of the Bible. The middle *him* in all the new modern versions of 1ˢᵗ John is changed to *child* in some versions, *children* in another, *whoever* in another, and *the one born* in another. Every change effects the story in some way, and that is really bad. I will focus on the story, and throughout this book read from the KJV, not for any other reason other than the newer versions are owned by publishing companies, and I have to ask their permission to write the truth if I use their product. The old version works just fine, and when it gets to old and ethy I will paraphrase.

The Holy Bible is a story, and that story is all tied together. The Old Testament all ties together, and the New Testament all ties together, and Jesus is the Link between the two. A major point of this little book is to show how the New Testament books are indeed all tied together as one story and how they all fit. The modern church would show them all bound neatly on one edge as they are and refer to that binding as the thread that takes all the books and ties them to Jesus. I'm saying every phrase in every book in the New Testament is tied to the next book, not by the thread in the binder, but more like a needle and thread piercing from one page to another and back to another. Not like a neat ball of yarn, but like a giant wad of tangled fishing line in a net, and the whole tackle box dumped on top, with gobs of sea weed mixed in and a big fish covered in sand flipping around like crazy. I will show an example. Mark leaves the mission field and writes a Gospel, and he ends it with a statement from Jesus that says snakes can't hurt you. Towards the end of Acts, Paul is bitten by a viper. Paul just shook it off in the fire and gave it no worry. A short while later while in Rome in chains, Paul has Timothy get Mark because he is useful for ministry. In the New Testament I'm reading, everything is connected. Not by a reference point or like verse, but by the story line, and evidence from the Word to confirm it.

The evidence for the Mark story is from the Bible, but you will be told it can't be true because some scholars believe the Gospel of Mark was written around AD 59 because of an opinion made by St. Irenaeus in *Adverse Heresies*. If you go to church long enough you will eventually hear the Bible story where Mark leaves the mission field because he is weak hearted and can't handle it. This is a made-up story from one pastor to another, and since it has a story line that everybody uses, well it must be true. The fact is there is no evidence in the Word of God to support this story for one second. There is evidence for the story of Paul and Mark, but it sure doesn't say that.

When you sit down with a good novel, you know that by the end, all the stories and happenings of the novel will come together and make sense. When the church reads the Word, they expect to locate another great verse. The books and letters of the New Testament are a novel, written by different authors, that in the end, all come together and make sense. To this point, most readers will agree, and that's just it: Because of preconceived scholarly opinions believed to be biblical beliefs, the church world and I finish the Word to a different ending. Therefore, I must take some time and show these preconceived opinions and attempt to erase them, so that you can see the stories in the New Testament. Thus, outside the Bible we go.

Letter

The Author

To my fellow readers seeking truth; Greetings

to be enlightened by the true wisdoms of the word of God, there are four sources one must be able to discern to achieve one's elevated state of knowledge.

with the correct knowledge, all things can be known, from the beginning to the end.

test all things and hold fast that which is good.

Amen

If this were in the front of the book, no one would read the book, because the letter is gobbley goo. It is a waste of words. It is true, but vague and obscure and incomplete. Yet, while in the pages of the book, and in reference to material as a training aid, it is very beneficial and eye opening. Even though the wording is dumb and gnostic like, because of that, specific ideas can be discussed, and will be. If the letter were presented outside the book it would have no value.

Yet, outside the book, scholars and historians, and commentators would source and date the work, and find several different possibilities as to whom the author is; by manuscript and style, which is a challenge, not knowing the original language and translation. But assuming it is Greek, and with a Gnostic flair, the odds of a 2nd Century author in the era of Valentinus would seem quite logical. A further study of the works of Irenaeus, show that, I hope by now you know that I'm just making stuff up. I'm the Author, duh. I hope you get my point. I will reference this dumb letter several times. As to the four sources of discernment; they are real, so let's get to number one.

2

FAIRY TALES

Sometimes it just doesn't work out like you think it should. He cast out one annoying demon and you think good job, right? Nope, drug before the magistrate, both of them whipped with rods for no reason, and shackled and locked in the dungeon with no good outcome in sight. Silas starts tapping a toe and the chains sound pretty cool, so just like it was orchestrated, they both break into song. The apostle's hittin' the deep low notes.

Open any study Bible to the Epistles of John and the very first thing you are going to see is the study guide which is often longer than the letters itself. Somewhere, if not all over these few paragraphs of wisdom on these three small Epistles will be the words, "John is writing to combat some early form of Gnosticism." They usually say that it's a form of Docetism or Cerinthianism. It doesn't matter which study Bible you have, it's in all of them. I have not found one yet that doesn't mention Gnosticism somewhere in the study guide sections in the New Testament. Some study Bibles go as far as taking the Gnostic thing clear into Colossians, and Galatians, and even 1st

Timothy. These pages in the study guides have become the belief of the Christian world.

When you approach any study materials on the Epistles of John, you are at the onslaught going to be taught that these writings were to combat Gnosticism. There are a couple newer study Bible versions that are doing away with the word Gnosticism and drifting toward Docetism, which is different, but to most Christians, this is still considered a form of Gnosticism. In the light of the information we have in this modern era, others are settling for just false teachings, and that has the same effect. The overall belief, still, is that John was confronting Gnosticism. Do you know why? Because scholars have no clue as to what the Epistles say.

The Creation of Bible Gnosis

There are no Gnostics in the Bible. None. To understand what the Word of God says, you must remove Gnostics from it. They are a real thing in the 2nd century, but in New Testament times they do not exist. A simple description of biblical Gnosticism is the blending of the coming of Jesus with religious beliefs of other Gentile nations. That's all. This didn't happen until the 2nd century, so all thought of combating Gnosticism in the Bible needs to be removed.

The creators of Gnosticism are in the Bible, but Paul and John are not promoting this work they started. Say what? Yes, Paul and John are the creators of Gnosticism. In biblical New Testament times, Gnosticism would be the blending of Greek theology with Christian religion, and Paul did just that. Paul preached to the philosophers in Athens, and he said, "I perceived that in all things ye are too superstitious. For as I passed by and beheld your devotions, I found an alter with this inscription, TO THE UNKNOWN GOD. Whom therefore ye ignorantly worship, him declare I unto you." KJV. And thus, with this act, tied Greek theology to Christ, making Paul an official Gnostic. And as for John, well let's see. "In the beginning was the Word, and the Word was with God, and the Word was God. The same was in the beginning with God. All things were made by Him, and without Him was not anything made that was made." KJV.

Is that not philosophical? If you look at the work of Valentinus, in *The Gospel of Truth*, you will see that Valentinus actually emulates the style of John with the repetition of metaphors. John writes, "In the beginning was the word...all things were made by him...In him was life... and the darkness comprehended it not." KJV. The gospel of truth follows this same pattern with the metaphors and use of the word *him*. It is obvious that this Roman Christian leader was influenced by the words of John. St. Irenaeus confirms this in his work. Valentinus is a 2nd century church leader that lived to approximately AD 160, way past New Testament times, and was truly a Gnostic. Some scholars say the writing of *The Gospel of Truth* is very likely the work of Valentinus. It's nice of some scholars to think that, because all known evidence points to Valentinus as the author. No evidence suggests Valentinus is not the author, and no evidence suggests it may have been penned by another author, or anybody else in any way. Thus, I say again, John and Paul are the creators of Gnosticism, but there are no Gnostics in the Bible. John and Paul's good works within one hundred years were twisted. But let's stay on point. There are no Gnostics in the Bible. Not one stitch. Not one line. They did not exist till post Bible book times. I know many millions of believers think it's there, but it's not.

Jesus said, beware of the Pharisees, the Sadducees and the Scribes. If you focus on every encounter the apostles have within the churches, it is with this group of people. The apostles fight is constantly with the church. Every fight outside the church is still instigated by Jews, except for that demon in the slave girl, and how did that turn out? Glorifying God!

Who is putting Gnosticism in the study Bible? Really! Academics would say I'm absolutely wrong. They would make reference to enaeus, from the 2nd century who wrote *Adverse Heresies*, in ongoing battle with Gnostics of different kinds. He categorizes ifferent sects and lists Simon the Sorcerer as the founder of ticism. His source for this information is from St. Justin, who letters of apologetics to Caesar, questions Caesar as to the ing for persecutions, and asks why would he build a statue to Simon? This all being proof of Gnosticism in the first century. Church history says that Nero brought Peter and Paul together with Simon for a show down, so Simon could prove he was greater. And in the presence of Nero and the multitude, Simon started levitating off the ground to prove his superiority, but Peter and Paul prayed and Simon fell and broke his neck and died. This upset Nero, so he had Peter and Paul killed. This is the proof that Gnostics did exist; and Humpty Dumpty sat on a wall.

In 1st Timothy when Paul wrote, "O Timothy, keep that which is committed to thy trust, avoiding profane and vain babblings, and oppositions of *science* falsely so called: which some professing have erred concerning the faith." KJV. That word *science*, in all the modern versions of 1st Timothy says knowledge. It is the correct modern translation for the Greek word gnosis. This is one of those places where those who believe in 1st century Gnosticism, say that Paul was confronting the subject because of "profane and vain babblings" that they pass for knowledge. The only way to consider that as a possibility is to study a verse, and not read the letter. What does the letter to Timothy say on this subject? Let's see. I've paraphrased the pertinent lines from the KJV text. Paul writes to Timothy, "As I requested you stay at Ephesus when I went to Macedonia, that you might instruct some that that they teach no other doctrine. Do not give heed to fables or endless genealogies which cause quarreling rather than Godly edification to our faith. The commandment is to love with a pure heart, with a good conscience and genuine faith, from which some have moved aside and turned to pointless arguments, desiring to be teachers of the law, understanding neither what they say nor what they believe." Then Paul writes, "Know that the law is not made for the righteous man, but for the lawless and disobedient, and for the ungodly and for sinners, the unholy and profane." Then Paul gave instruction that through the prophesies Timothy has already received, that he should fight the good fight, having faith and a good conscience, which some have already lost and suffered shipwreck. Then Paul writes, "These are Hymenaeus and Alexander, whom I have delivered to Satan that they may learn not to blaspheme." He writes, "The Spirit clearly says that in the latter times some will depart from the faith, giving heed to seducing spirits and doctrines of devils, speaking lies in hypocrisy, having their conscience seared with a hot iron." He then says to refuse profane and old wives' fables, and work towards godliness. Then Paul goes on to write, that the widows have become idle, wandering from house to house being trouble makers and busybodies, saying things they shouldn't. Therefore, he writes that the younger widows should marry, and because of their idleness some have turned to Satan. He says to teach and exhort these things. Then he writes, "If anyone teach otherwise, and does not agree to the wholesome words of our Lord Jesus Christ, and to the doctrine that is of God, he is proud and knows nothing, cherishing the arguments to questions and words, whereof come, envy, strife, railings, and evil surmising. These are perverse disputing's of men of corrupt minds and destitute of the truth, supposing that gain is Godliness." These he says to avoid. And still paraphrased, Paul writes, "But you O man of God, flee these things and follow after righteousness, godliness, faith, love, patience and meekness." And in summary he writes, "O Timothy, keep what was committed to your trust by avoiding profane and vain babblings, and contradictions that are passed as knowledge, which some profess and have become lost concerning the faith."

In this short description of 1st Timothy, the fables and endless genealogies and the teachers of the law are the Pharisees, Sadducees, and the Scribes no doubt. Gossiping widows that are busybodies and trouble makers are an issue. Paul defines the situations in the letter, and then he says, avoid the profane and vain babblings of what is falsely called knowledge. 1st Timothy is a short letter with instruction for Timothy to combat the Pharisees, Sadducees, and the Scribes, and their effects on the people of the church. In a well written and directed letter where Paul has already tossed out Hymenaeus and Alexander and says that the arguments are about endless genealogies and the law, just guarantees the problems are with the Pharisees, Sadducees, and Scribes. Those denying Jesus as Christ through genealogy and enforcing the law of Moses are not Gnostics. Their knowledge is called Judaism. They are the one's Jesus warned about. But scholars through all their wisdom see Gnostics.

Let me tell a story. There has been a murder in your community. Three separate witnesses of good character have testified that they saw the accused leaving the vicinity of the crime at the time of the incident. Furthermore, the fingerprint of the accused is on the knife blade in the victim's blood and is confirmed the murder weapon. The blood of the victim was found on the clothes of the accused at the residence where the arrest was made. The accused has been known to carry a knife just like the one used in the incident. All solid direct evidence suggests that the accused is guilty beyond a shadow of a doubt. However, at the trial, the defense introduces a new witness. A friend of the accused has a verifiable alibi to his whereabouts at the time of the incident and swears under oath that the accused was with him at this time. Because of this alibi, the prosecuting attorney requires the police to dig deeper and see if they missed anything. They comb this section of the community and discover a man with similar features and build as the accused and made the connection that they shop at the same grocery store. Also, they discovered this new perpetrator is of a nationality different than that of the community and was once seen protesting by that same store. The knife used in the murder was made in the country that the new perpetrator is from. This bad guy has no verifiable alibi to his whereabouts at the time of the murder. Charges are brought against this man and he is soon found guilty by a jury of his peers. The evidence against the first guy can't be used by default, because he was found innocent and released.

Does that sound dumb? Well compare it to this. That's a made-up story and this is truth. I have to prove that Gnosticism is not in the Bible by quoting and referencing what is not there. There is a culprit and he is well defined, but he walks freely, while the Gnostics, who at this time don't exist are convicted of all malicious acts. In 1st Timothy, Paul is telling Timothy what to prepare for, and that they pass this for knowledge. Oh, the bad word, and surely a sign. This is sarcasm on my part, but it's just as pertinent as the bad guy shopping at the same grocery store. Timothy is told to avoid arguments of endless genealogies and wives' fables, so who would worry about endless genealogies? For a hint check out the book of Numbers, or the book of 1st Chronicles. That's more sarcasm, obviously, it is the Pharisees, Sadducees and Scribes. The Gospel of Matthew is believed to be the first Gospel written and it starts with the genealogy of Joseph, the husband of Mary, who is the mother of Jesus. Joseph's genealogy goes through the king's lineage and oops, it goes right through Jeconiah. God told the prophet Jeremiah, that nothing would go through the seed of Jeconiah. So see, the Sadducees say that Jesus can only be a prophet, and not the Son of God. Don't worry though, Joseph is not the father of Jesus. He's just the dad.

And as for old wives' tales, well, let me tell you one. Sure, Jesus was a righteous man, and when John the Baptist baptized Him, the Spirit of God in the form of Christ came upon him. He did many great signs and wonders. (That is the gospel of Cerinthus as learned from Irenaeus) Then this prophet began speaking of riches in heaven and confused the multitude which caused an uproar, so Pilate had him crucified, and the spirit of Christ was released from this mad man. After his death, some of his closest followers continued with his message in hopes of taking over the temple and the authority of God's people. Their whole goal is to undermine the laws of Moses with their crazy talk of going to heaven and living with God. See, in Paul's day, that is what the old covenant religion claimed of Christianity. That was the theme of the wives' fables and the people Paul was fighting were Jews. Jesus said, beware of the

Pharisees, Sadducees and the Scribes over and over. And not once ever did He say beware of the Gnostics.

When the letters of the apostles are said to be written to combat Gnostics, which is absolutely untrue, the message of the Bible gets changed. If the courts wrongfully convict an innocent man of murder, and he is tried and hung and justice is served, isn't the murderer still among us? The apostles were writing to warn against this murderer. Instead we have tried and convicted someone else for the crime and embrace the actual murderer. When you believe Gnosticism is the reason for the letters, you cannot see, **CANNOT SEE** the actual intent of the letters. When you remove the fictitious mythical Gnosticism from the Bible, the real murderer is standing there smiling.

Some intellectual about a hundred years ago, linked the writings of the 2nd century saints, and the folk lore of the day, and searched the King James Version for clues to tie the stories together and hence, installed the possibility of Gnosticism in the Bible. At that time, there was not sufficient evidence to refute such a story. However, with the information available today, this story line is incorrect and null and void because of hard evidence that can be compiled by anyone willing to look. St. Justin was wrong about the statue of Simon, and this is where St. Irenaeus acquired his information on Simon, making his assessment on the origination of Gnosticism just another fable. The stories told through the ages are just stories, and Gnosticism is not in the Bible. As for the King James or any other Bible, there are no Gnostics. Every scripture or verse that is attributed to Gnosticism, with just a little study of the letter, will show that the problem addressed is with the Pharisees, Sadducees and the Scribes.

From the writings of St. Irenaeus, the present-day Christian world believes that Gnostics are in the Bible, and I'm telling you, **stop it**.

I must Kill Cerinthus

The most notorious make-believe Gnostic in the Bible is Cerinthus. I decided I have to kill Cerinthus and it's like killing the tooth fairy. Wikipedia says, "In northern Europe there was a tradition of *tand-fe*' or tooth fee, which was paid when a child lost their first tooth. This tradition is recorded in writings as early as Eddas, which are the earliest written Norse and Northern European traditions." History says it's a real thing and scholars study the practice. The next line from Wikipedia says, "The reward left varies by Country, the family's economic status, the amounts the child's peers report receiving and other factors. A 2013 survey by Visa Inc. found that American children receive $3.70 per tooth on average." This is circumstantial evidence that the tooth fairy exists. Now, I hope you're not offended, but the tooth fairy is not real. The parents of the child put that money under the pillow and remove the extracted tooth. There is no tooth fairy. As an adult you know that. For me to kill the tooth fairy, I have to show the real culprit. In this case it is the parent. To show the real culprit in the New Testament I have to kill Cerinthus, and like the tooth fairy, there is nothing to kill. Oh, there are tidbits of scholarly information with big words that mean nothing, that can be refuted for indefinite illogical realms of probable doubt, but the fact is Cerinthus is just like, I repeat, "just like" the tooth fairy. He is not the enemy of the New Testament. Cerinthus is just part of the alibi for the real enemy.

In approximately AD 170, St. Irenaeus wrote a book of worthy arguments against the Gnostics of his time, being mostly the followers of Valentinus and Marcion. He states very clearly in *Adverse Heresies* (book 3, chapter 4, number 3), that these groups had no existence prior to their founder's existence which is 2nd century. He says the rest of the Gnostics come from Menander, the descendant of Simon. He says the descendants of Menander, were active during the immediate period of the church. The evidence for this comes from St. Justin

Martyr. In his first apology to the Emperor, addressed to, Titus Aelius Andianus Antoninus Pius Augustus Caesar, Justin writes,

> "There was a Samaritan, Simon, a native of the village called Gitto, who in the reign of Claudius Caesar, and in your royal city of Rome, did mighty acts of magic, by virtue of the art of the devils operating in him. He was considered a god, and as a god was honored by you with a statue, which statue was erected on the river Tiber, between the two bridges, and bore this inscription, in the language of Rome: "Simoni Deo Sancto", "To Simon the Holy God.""

This had to make Caesar shake his head in confusion, because, see, St. Justin was mis-informed. There was a statue on the Tiber between the two bridges that was built several hundred years before Christ, and it was built to Simon, yes, Simon the accountant. The Christian missionaries that reported this injustice to St. Justin were wrong. This is the total solid evidence for Simon. The rest is folk lore built on this false truth. The Bible says Simon repented. Luke wrote this. Luke also finished the same book from Rome. If these events had any truth Luke would have made note. In the space of nothing, because the Bible says Simon repented, we have one hundred and twenty years later, Irenaeus writing the history of Simon. In *Adverse Heresies* (book 1, chapter 23, number 1), he tells the story of Simon through the book of Acts 8:9-11. Then he writes,

> "This Simon, then- who feigned faith, supposing that the Apostles themselves performed their cures by the art of magic, and not by the power of God; and with to their filling with the Holy Ghost through the imposition of hands, those that believed in God through Him who was preached by them, namely, Christ Jesus- suspecting that even this was

done through a kind of greater knowledge of magic, and offering money to the Apostles, thought he, too, might receive this power of bestowing the Holy Spirit on whomsoever he would- was addressed in these words by Peter:"

Then Irenaeus quotes Acts 8:21-23, which says, "Your money perish with you, because you have thought that the gift of God can be purchased with money: you have neither part nor lot in this matter, for your heart is not right in the sight of God; for I perceive that you are in the gall of bitterness, and in the bond of iniquity." (Translation by Phillip Schaff in Adverse Heresies) Irenaeus then writes,

"He, then not putting faith in God a whit the more, set himself eagerly to contend against the Apostles, in order that he himself might seem to be a wonderful being, and applied himself with still greater zeal to the study of the whole magic art, that he might the better bewilder and overpower multitudes of men. Such was his procedure in the reign of Claudius Caesar, by whom also he is said to have been honored with a statue, on account of his magical power."

What Irenaeus never wrote was the very next verse in Acts which says, "Then answered Simon, and said, pray ye to the Lord for me, that none of these things which ye have spoken come upon me." KJV. Simon repented! There is no evidence that proves anything else about Simon. The rest is folk lore.

The evidence from Irenaeus is based on evidence from Justin that is based on evidence of a statue that we absolutely know is false. Gnosticism is not a real thing in New Testament times. So how do I kill Cerinthus?

All that we know about Cerinthus is from Irenaeus, and it is without source other than Irenaeus. Let's examine some more folklore as it comes from Irenaeus in a story from *Adverse Heresies* (book 3, chapter 3, number 4). It tells the story that John entered a bathhouse in Ephesus with his followers, and Cerinthus was there so he fled, saying, "Let us fly, lest even the bath house fall down, because Cerinthus, the enemy of truth is within." Now Irenaeus starts this writing with proof and truth of St. Polycarp, but before this story ends, proof and truth change to, "There are also those who heard from him that John ...," and then the story of the bath house. So now several generations pass and we have as evidence, that Irenaeus said, that someone said, that Polycarp said, that John said this. This is folk lore.

In *Adverse Heresies* (book 1, chapter 26, number 1), Irenaeus describes the beliefs of Cerinthus. It basically says Jesus was a man of Joseph and Mary, that He was more righteous, prudent, and wiser than other men, and at His baptism, Christ descended on Him in the form of a dove and left Him before crucifixion. Then Jesus died and rose again. In this description of Cerinthus' belief, there was a power above God the Father, and without this part applied, well, this would just be Judaism, which is what it was. The sad fact is there is no evidence for Cerinthus outside Irenaeus who is one hundred years outside New Testament times.

Another sad fact is a lot of what is preached as historical biblical evidence of the Gospels comes from *Adverse Heresies* by Irenaeus, and sadly, a lot of it is speculation by Irenaeus that scholars have turned into facts. I will give you some examples, but bear in mind that we only take the ones we like. In *Adverse Heresies* (book 3, chapter 1, number 1), Irenaeus writes,

> "Matthew also issued a written Gospel among the
> Hebrews in their own dialect, while Peter and Paul
> were preaching in Rome, and laying the foundations

of the church. After their departure, Mark the disciple and interpreter of Peter, did also hand down to us in writing what had been preached by Peter. Luke also, the companion of Paul, recorded in a book the gospel preached by him. Afterwards, John, the disciple of the Lord, who also had leaned on His breast, did himself publish a Gospel during his residence at Ephesus in Asia."

This is the evidence for the order of the Gospels in the scholastic world. From this proof that Irenaeus writes, he is able to make the tale of Cerinthus a foe of John, and scholars know this must be true because this is proven in the book *Adverse Heresies*, where we learned that Polycarp said so. As already noted, (book 3, chapter 3, number 4), Irenaeus writes a beautiful eulogy to Polycarp and then writes, "There are also those that heard from him that John, the disciple of the Lord, going to bathe at Ephesus, and perceiving Cerinthus within, rushed out of the bath house without bathing, exclaiming, 'Let us fly...'" Therefore, the evidence of scholars that John and Cerinthus are in the same region and in the same era is proven by Polycarp. But did you catch the scholar's evidence? Irenaeus said, that someone said, that Polycarp said, that John said, "Let us fly..." To make his point, Irenaeus used the strength of the witness of Polycarp and the folklore of the saints for the evidence to his case. Some people said that Polycarp said is scholarly evidence that John wrote his gospel to confront Cerinthus. This can only be proven by the book *Adverse Heresies* (book 3, chapter 11, number 1), where Irenaeus writes, "John, the disciple of the Lord, preaches this faith, and seeks, by the proclamation of the Gospel, to remove that error which by Cerinthus had been disseminated among men..." And along with the book, again in *Adverse Heresies* (book 3, chapter 1, number 1), it says John wrote his book in Ephesus, and that is where the scholars rest their case. To scholars this evidence is irrefutable, because there is no other evidence to refute this evidence of Cerinthus.

In *Adverse Heresies* (book 2, chapter 22, number 5 and 6), in the argument to prove that Jesus preached after baptism for more than twelve months, and did not suffer in the twelfth month, as some Gnostic groups claimed, Irenaeus made a very strong case. He writes in number 5,

> "Now, that the first of early life embraces thirty years, and that this extends onwards to the fortieth year, anyone will admit; but from the fortieth and fiftieth year a man begins to decline towards old age, which our Lord possessed while He still fulfilled the office of a teacher, even as the Gospel and all the elders testify; those who were conversant in Asia with John, the disciple of the Lord,[affirming] that John conveyed to them that information. And He remained among them up to the times of Trajan."

Trajan was born September, 18, in AD 53, so Jesus was in His mid-fifties before He suffered. The next sentence says, "Some of them moreover, saw not only John, but the other apostles also, and heard the very same account from them, and bear testimony as to the [validity of] the statement." This issue of age is confirmed by Irenaeus in number 6, with biblical evidence and logic to prove Jesus was at least fifty when He suffered. Please note that this last truth from Irenaeus to prove his case, has evidence not only from John, but other apostles as well, and is supported by doctrine in John 8:56-57, with solid logic to support the doctrine. Where are the scholars? The amount of evidence for this point is double that of the other issues, and the scholars conveniently missed it.

Everything we know for Cerinthus came from *Adverse Heresies*, and without the book, he does not exist. Everything Irenaeus knew of this fellow came from word of mouth, and the simple truth is that there is more factual evidence for the tooth fairy than for Cerinthus. Irenaeus wrote that John wrote his Gospel to remove the error of Cerinthus, so scholars say that John wrote his Epistles to fight Gnosticism. The whole of Gnosticism comes from Irenaeus as well as much other scholastic knowledge for the Bible. The sad, sad fact of the matter is scholars use information that meets their agenda. The same author from the same book that scholars make their whole argument of Gnostics in the Bible from, ignore the facts that the evidence is mere opinion and hear say, and when the evidence points to something else like Jesus being over fifty years old, they just ignore it.

All we know of Cerinthus comes from Irenaeus, and all of it is questionable at best. He says that Valentinus and Marcion are 2nd century only. He says the Menander's go back to Simon because there's a statue. And he says that John wrote his Gospel to fight the Gnosticism of Cerinthus, that by Irenaeus' description is just the argument of the Pharisees, Sadducees, and Scribes with a Gnostic flair added for flavor. Gnosticism in the New Testament is based on this, and it's nothing. Like the tooth fairy, it's made up. Sure, it's a real thing in Irenaeus's time, and his battle is real with Valentinus and Marcion, but the rest is just creative writing. In modern times we call it fiction. And just like the tooth fairy, at a certain age you are told or discover the truth, and you never look back and say, "It could be the tooth fairy and not my parents that put that dollar under my pillow." At some point in this little book, if not already, you will discover that Gnostics do not exist in the New Testament, and the enemy is the Pharisees, Sadducees, and Scribes. I really don't want to lose anyone on this point, and I understand that it is ingrained as a thing in modern Christian theology, so I beg you to bear with me. Soon the idea of John battling Gnostics in his letters will disappear.

It's not my position or intention to beat up my brother, St. Irenaeus. We both work for Jesus Christ, and I just have more access to information than him. We have a lot in common. We are both writing books to expose the truth. Some things in our style are the same. We both aggressively expose untruth and share a flair for sarcastic aggression toward the foe. My brother has no problem saying someone is insufficient in the brain. I love that stuff. He is doing everything possible in his writings to prove that Gnosticism in the 2nd century is the true enemy to Christianity in the region and time he is in. I agree with his sentiment. He is close to one hundred years out from any information on or about John, and what he has and uses is speculation. He does a great job with it and he paints a picture that on face value appears true. Every scholar has fed off his opinions as biblical evidence. Sadly, he is the only evidence, and it's professional opinion one hundred years out, and it's wrong on the points covered. How do I know? The Bible says so. Just like with the tooth fairy, when you understand the truth of the Bible, the other stories are just stories. I hope to meet Irenaeus some day, and it will be laughter and high fives. But let's face it, without Irenaeus there is no Cerinthus. Mind you that my brother believes what he is writing! This tells me that some of the truth of the history of the Gospels is already lost.

Everything we know about Gnostics in the Bible came from Irenaeus, and I don't care if one hundred million scholars believe he is correct, he's not. You read four more chapters and you'll know they're wrong too. Or you'll be trying to find a way to prove I'm unqualified to understand the complexities of the garbage being passed as knowledge. I'm not the one insufficient in the brain!

I was searching for proof on 1st John using Google, and it hooked me up with a professor's blog from Dallas Seminary. He gave every piece of information available to humankind that could prove the location of the writing of John's letters. Everything he had was opinion and wrong. How do I know? I read the Bible. We say we believe the Bible to be the true word of God, but this scholar took maybe ten pieces of evidence all from outside the Bible and made his conclusion. What about Bible evidence? In 1st John it says if we have the witness of men, the witness of God is greater, and scholars don't even look at the Book! We don't study the letter through the pen of John, because we are too busy in the study of the letter through the knowledge of scholars. Do you trust the word of God? Do you!

Here is a hard question. Why does your church insist Gnostics have to be there? Academia is slowly adjusting its view. The availability of manuscripts from the Nag Hamadi, and the ease of access to information from the internet on the subject, make truth available, but still old teachings have their hold, and will take time to dismantle. The church tries to modify the definition of Gnosticism to encompass all heresy, and that way it's still in the Bible. But we can easily distinguish with just a little study, that what Paul is fighting is Judaism. You pick any letter from Paul, and with study, it's easy to see that it's always Judaism. And in the Epistles of John it's the same thing. But wait, "most scholars", yea, "most scholars say," in fact, "almost all scholars say," John wrote his Epistles when he was ninety years old, at the turn of the century, and that he was battling Gnosticism. Wouldn't that be a more logical enemy at that time? And that brings us to discernment number two.

3

DEJA VU

Barnabas and Luke are staring at him like he's a lunatic. They stoned him to death in Lystra and drug him to the edge of the city like a dead dog, and now he's saying let's go minister to them? The apostle smiles with his freshly stone-beaten face and says, "I once was the rock thrower and look at the love the Lord has for me." They chuckle and head back to the battle ground.

Most scholars believe that the three Epistles of John were written when John was an old man at the end of the first century. Almost all study Bibles will say something to the fact that one of the founding fathers said that John wrote the letters as an old man after his release from Patmos and that he wrote the letters to combat early Gnosticism. The list they give as evidence is nothing more than hopeful circumstance on their part. Read close because it will say that some Saint said so and so, and then scholars add something else, and that's the evidence. As further evidence, scholars say John never mentions the destruction of the temple in Jerusalem, so the writings must be much older than AD 70. Think about that. If something is not mentioned in a pointed letter, then it's evidence in favor of the scholars' opinion. That is stupid. John was not writing about destruction. He was writing about love for your brother. That's like saying I failed to mention the winter Olympics in Korea, so my writing of this book must be at a later date. But it's really like I forgot to mention the 2024 summer Olympics, so it must be much later. I failed to mention the future, so the time must be further in the future? That's what the scholars' logic has done.

The fact of the matter is that all sources on the subject say the same thing. They say that John was in his nineties when he wrote the three Epistles. Most scholars agree that the Epistles were written at the end of the first century in an effort to combat Gnosticism. All solid evidence for this belief equals nothing. The evidence is all suggestive and imaginary. There is real evidence in the Word of God for the time frame of John's letters, but it all has been overridden by scholarly belief.

Remember the little letter I wrote right before chapter two. I said there are four sources one must be able to discern. The first was fictitious Gnosticism, and now the second is the time of John's Epistles. To achieve an elevated state of knowledge, one must know that there are no Gnostics in the Bible, and that the Epistles of John were written in the late fifties, not the nineties. John wouldn't mention the devastation of the temple in the seventies, in a letter he wrote before it happened. Yet, scholars insist on AD 90 by the evidence he didn't mention.

With the correct knowledge, all things can be known. Test all things, hold fast that which is good. Amen.

Like Gnosticism, this late dating is a barrier to the truth. It has been placed there by academia and is something that needs to be removed. It is wrong. Gnosticism is harder to disprove, because there is nothing to disprove, but rather one must show the actual enemy.

However, the date of John's letters is actually fun to prove, because there is biblical evidence that cannot be logically denied. The only problem is first eliminating all the scholarly evidence that doesn't exist. So here we go.

This is what the study Bibles build their belief on. The evidence presented for the three Epistles to be written by old man John in his nineties at the turn of the century.

The arguments made by scholars are:

- John refers to himself as elder.
- He refers to the letter recipients as little children.
- The writings are elegant and mature in nature.
- St. Eusebius stated that John was freed from exile on the Island of Patmos.
- St. Clement of Alexandria stated that John spent his final years ministering to the churches in Asia.
- The letters failed to mention the destruction of the temple in Jerusalem in AD 70.
- The first known record of the letters was in Asia.
- There is no record of earlier use of the Epistles.
- Cerinthus is a known adversary of John.
- John never mentions what ism he is combating, so it must be Gnosticism.
- The whole church believes that these Epistles were written by old man John while he was in Asia to combat Gnosticism.

All this evidence is called overwhelming, and conclusive, and undeniable and whatever other word you want to use to show that it's a sure thing, but it's not. All this evidence is circumstantial, and most of the circumstances are true, but it does not prove that John was in his nineties when he wrote the Epistles.

In 3rd John, John refers to himself as the elder. Gaius would understand from this short greeting that he was dealing with John the apostle, the one Jesus loved the most, Bergones, the son of thunder, he who was with Jesus from the beginning, and his friend. There was nothing to do with age. If you look at it, Paul refers to both Timothy and Titus as *sons in faith*. From the letters to these younger men, we know they had the authority not only to appoint elders but also to hold them accountable. It has nothing to do with age. But we're not dealing with any elder. This letter is from *the elder*. *The elder,* is a metaphor for the apostle John, just like *sons in faith* is a metaphor for Timothy and Titus, who were brought to the faith by Paul, and now are fellow workers. There is no proof by this word elder, that John is ninety years old.

In 3rd John, He refers to Gaius as one of my children. This suggests that Gaius was brought to the family of Jesus by John. How does that make him ninety years old? It doesn't. And if it comes to the point, that the quality of the writing gets to depict your age, well duh, then I'm fifteen. And St. Eusebius said John was freed from his exile on the island of Patmos. Okay, how does that prove that he wrote the letters upon his freedom? It doesn't. And St. Clement of Alexandria said that John spent his later years ministering to the churches of Asia. Okay, how does that prove he wrote the letters while he was there. It doesn't. The letters failed to mention the destruction of Jerusalem. It hadn't been destroyed yet. The first known record of the Epistles was in Asia, at Ephesus. That makes perfect sense. Does that make John ninety years old when he wrote it? No. And, there are no earlier record of the Epistles. Well let's see; a personal letter to Gaius, and a personal letter to the elect lady, with no attributes to Jesus that would even give them reason to be in the Bible, and you expect them to be quoted by the masses as scripture? Think about it! Yea, but what about 1st John? That's just it, when you know who your brother is and the letter makes total sense, well, then it becomes a different thing, not a letter for the masses, so keep reading. The letters were not written to the masses for edification. There should be no record of early use of the Epistles, and it doesn't make John ninety when he wrote them. And Cerinthus is a known adversary of John. Okay, as suggested by Irenaeus, Cerinthus preached that Christ was a spirit that came upon Jesus at baptism and left at crucifixion, making Jesus just a man. That is not Gnosticism. That is Judaism, making Jesus just another prophet. And John never mentions exactly what he's combating. He does. You just can't see it yet. And the whole church, and all of history says John wrote it while he was ninety to combat Gnosticism. What does the Bible say?

Just like the evidence for the conviction in the made-up murder story, the evidence for the date of the Epistles of John that says they were written at the turn of the century is all circumstantial without one piece of solid physical evidence. St. Eusebius didn't say John left Patmos and then he wrote his letters. He said John left Patmos, and scholars said, "and it's obvious he wrote his letters then". Circumstantial evidence is good stuff, but it has to align with all the other truths or it is contradictory, and might just be circumstantial, and not evidence at all, but just rather coincidental. In the made-up murder story, it's obvious the first accused is guilty, except for the alibi from one person, which questions all the direct evidence, so the second bad guy gets convicted on circumstantial evidence. That evidence was that he shops at the same grocery store, and he protested once at that store, and he's from a different region, and the knife was from that region, and he had no verifiable alibi. See, this can be called circumstantial evidence, but really, it's just coincidental. It's easy to see that it's coincidental because we know the direct evidence all points to the first accused. The same thing happens with the circumstantial evidence that makes the Epistles from the turn of the century. When you see the direct evidence that says they are from the AD 50's all that circumstantial evidence becomes coincidental. Solid biblical evidence says the letters are from a very specific time. The evidence is overwhelming, except for the alibi from scholars that say the Epistles of John were written around AD 90.

It's obvious that scholars don't believe the Bible to be a historical document, and somehow, they think it is not a legitimate source of evidence. However, I believe the story of the Bible to be the Word of God and historically accurate. If you are not a believer in the Word, I know you can see the evidence about to be presented. But, if you are one of those like me who say, "I believe the Bible to be the true Word of God," then I'm believing that the evidence in the Word of God must be true to you as well. Or are you believing scholars?

As evidence, I present to you:

The Third Epistle of John

> The Elder unto the well-beloved Gaius, whom I love in the truth.
>
> Beloved, I wish above all things that thou mayest prosper and be in health, even as thy soul prospereth. For I rejoiced greatly, when the brethren came and testified of the truth that is in thee, even as thou walkest in the truth. I have no greater joy than to hear that my children walk in truth. Beloved thou doest faithfully whatsoever thou doest to the brethren and strangers; which have born witness of thy charity before the church: Whom if thou bring forward on their journey after a godly sort, thou shall do well: Because that for His name's sake they went forth taking nothing from the Gentiles. We therefore ought to receive such, that we might be fellow helpers to the truth.
>
> I wrote unto the church: but Diotrephes, who loveth to have the preeminence among them, receiveth us not. Wherefore, if I come, I will remember his deeds which he doeth, prating against us with malicious

words: and not content therewith, neither doth he himself receive the brethren, and forbiddeth them that would, and casteth them out of the church.

Beloved, follow not that which is evil, but that which is good. He that doeth good is of God: but he that doeth evil hath not seen God. Demetrius hath good report of all men, and of the truth itself: yea, and we also bear record; and ye know that our record is true.

I had many things to write, but I will not with ink and pen write unto thee: but I trust I shall shortly see thee, and we shall speak face to face. Peace be to thee. Our friends salute thee. Greet the friends by name. KJV.

There are keys in the Bible to help us understand what it says. 2nd and 3rd John are only in the Bible for this reason. I know most scholars and most readers will not agree with me, but after the next little bit of reading, you may want to change your mind.

By canon standards, why are 2nd and 3rd John in the Bible? They meet no canon criteria. Where is the enlightenment of Jesus in these books? By my limited knowledge on the subject, I think the rules for canonization are that it needs to be spirit-filled and should be manifesting Jesus to all who read. This is not present in the letter to the elect lady and Gaius. The main theme is, I see your children walking in faith, and don't let the bad guys in your house, see ya soon. Sorry, but that's not canonable. So why is it here? Because they are the keys to understanding 1st John. They are the keys to understanding who your brother is. Let's look at the truths in 3rd John as evidence for John's writings being in the late fifties.

REAL EVIDENCE

In approximately AD 57, Paul was returning to Jerusalem from his third missionary journey. Upon his arrival, he and his group met with James and all the elders, and he told them in detail those things which God had done among the Gentiles through his ministry.

It is obvious beyond a shadow of doubt that John was present as an elder at this meeting by truths in 3rd John. I will start with this outline of truths.

1. All the elders were present, and John addresses his letters as the elder.
   a. After Paul's first missionary journey, He and Barnabas were sent to Jerusalem to meet with the apostles and elders concerning the circumcision of Gentiles, as told in the story in Acts.
   b. From the letter to Galatians, we know that John was present then and was perceived as a pillar.
   c. Luke wrote both accounts of the meetings with the elders and would not have said all were present if John was not there.
2. John writes his letter to Gaius.
   a. Paul would have surely told in detail that his host in Macedonia was Gaius, which would give John joy in hearing that his children are walking in truth, and being a reason for the letter.
3. The Gaius that John writes to is hosting the brethren.
   a. In Paul's letter to the Romans, He says, Gaius, is his host and the host of the whole church, and this shows that he wrote that Epistle while he was at Gaius's home.
   b. Later, when Paul wrote 2nd Corinthians, he said that while he was with them and in need, that he was burden to no one because the brethren from Macedon supplied what he lacked. That was Gaius.

4. John said that the brethren testified of Gaius.
   a. Luke was at the meeting with Paul making the testimony plural.
   b. Demetrius knew Gaius and would have been at the meeting along with Paul's other traveling companions.
      a. Aristarchus is one of those traveling companions that knows Gaius.
      b. Tychicus, Timothy, Trophimus, and more were traveling with Paul, and they know Gaius.
5. Diotrephes is not accepting the brethren.
   a. Paul would have just told John about how he was turned around in Athens to avoid ambush and feared entering Ephesus, and Gaius was familiar with all the churches Paul was building. Obviously, Gaius knows Diotrephes.
   b. John tells Gaius that he wrote to the church that Diotrephes attends.
   c. John wrote 2nd John at the same time, and some of the traveling companions of Paul are from this Church.
6. Demetrius has a good report to tell.
   a. Just a handful of months earlier while Paul was in Ephesus, Gaius and Aristarchus, Paul's traveling companions from Macedonia, were dragged into the coliseum by Demetrius and his mob in a rage over Paul's works.
      a. That is one awesome testimony, surely spurring John to write that you may prosper in all things and health just as your soul prospers.
7. John writes, "I hope to see you shortly," which shows that John was planning to visit.
   a. From St. Eusebius and St. Clement of Alexandria we know that John spent his latter years ministering in Asia, which is right next door.
8. John says that our friends greet you, and to greet the friends by name, which shows some of the same precautionary practices John displays in the other two Epistles.

a. If no names are mentioned, no individual may be persecuted.

b. Friends would be the traveling party of Paul. They would also be the ones to deliver the letter to Gaius.

c. The idea of protection from persecution would be fresh on everybody's mind with the fact that just days ago, Paul was dragged from the temple, beaten, and arrested for no other charge other than his insistence that Jesus rose from the dead and is God.

d. The people who instigated the assault on Paul are Jews from Ephesus, and we know Paul had to backtrack out of Greece because Jews there were plotting against him.

9. The book of Acts could not have been finished until Paul was in Rome for at least two years, and it took several years to get there, so John could not have received a copy of this work for at least five years.

a. The letters of John were written before the book of Acts, making Acts a later confirmation.

10. The other two Epistles of John support the time frame.

Evidence that appeared to be circumstantial when standing on its own, now when applied to the story, is direct evidence for the early date. John refers to himself as the elder, and all the elders were present. Direct and circumstantial evidence support this. Proof 1. John writes his letter to Gaius, who is in Macedonia. There is solid Bible evidence to show this. All other direct and circumstantial evidence support this. Proof 2. Gaius in Macedonia is hosting and caring for the brethren. Solid evidence from Romans and 2nd Corinthians shows this. Proof 3. John said the brethren testified of Gaius, and Paul brought a whole crowd with him that had stayed at Gaius's home, or had benefited from his generosity. Proof 4. John said they didn't have to take from the Gentiles, and that's just what Paul said the Macedonians did. Proof 5. John said that Demetrius has a good report of all, and we know that in Ephesus, it was Gaius and Aristichus that Demetrius had drug into the theatre to be harmed or possibly killed. Aristichus is a traveler with Paul. Well, that makes awesome testimony. Proof 6. Diotrophes is not accepting the brethren, fits well, as we know that the Jews in Greece were plotting against Paul. Gaius is in that region, and obviously knows both Demetrius and Diotrophes. Proof 7. Knowing that those who took in the brethren would be removed from the church, and the fact that Paul just went to prison for believing that Jesus rose from the dead, shows the reason for 2nd John to be written with no names attached. Proof 8. 1st John supports this time frame, and that will soon be shown. Proof 9. All direct and circumstantial evidence from the New Testament stories agree with this time period for the writing of the three Epistles, and nothing contradicts the time period. Proof 10. Knowing that Luke was present at the meeting with all the elders and writes the book of Acts with all the mention and emphasis that ties to the story of the three Epistles is proof that John was there. The book was directed to him. This makes the date of AD 57 correct. Proof 11.

In this letter to Gaius, there is nothing in the story about Jesus. There is nothing spirit-filled. I'm not much of a football fan, but let's talk football for a moment. Let's talk about the 49ers. They've had some great players over the years. Joe Montana sticks out, and so does Steve Young. Two quarterbacks sure to go down in history as all-time greats. But I'll tell you, neither of them compares to the receiver that helped carry both of them to their greatness. That's right. Without Jerry Rice, they're both just another quarter back. And there you have a football story with opinion from me. I need to check these men's bios and see if they all believe in Jesus. I wrote this story and I believe in Jesus. And now this story is as spirit-filled as 2nd and 3rd John. I hope you get my point. 2nd and 3rd John don't belong in the Bible for any other reason than to show the way to 1st John. Knowing that 1st John was written in AD 57 can be proven by 3rd John. 3rd John shows that it was written at the time of Paul's return from his third missionary journey.

Look at the Odds

Let me prove this in another way. When I was searching for the truth in Christ, I read several books. My favorite authors were Lee Strobel and Josh McDowell. In Lee's proof for creation, he borrowed from Josh the story of how he hired a mathematician, and then took all the proofs for God, did the math, and showed the astronomical odds as proof. In that light, I shall proceed. I'm not hiring a mathematician, I'm just going to use some odds most can understand and call it good enough.

These are solid proofs from the Word. One, John is the elder, and all the elders were present. Two, John wrote Gaius of the Bible in Macedonia. Three, is Gaius took in the Brethren. Four, is Gaius supplied the needs of the brethren in Corinth so they took nothing from the Gentiles. Five, is the brethren testified and we can name them. Six, is the Demetrius in the Bible knows Gaius of Macedonia. Seven, is John knows that Gaius knows Diotrephes and would be aware of the situation and the reason for his coming. Eight, is that Luke writes about Gaius and Demetrius at a later date, and the story fits the letter of 3rd John. So what are the odds of John calling himself the elder, for the title of the letter, instead of say, the son of thunder, or the one Jesus loved the most, or the apostle or the apostle that leaned on Jesus breast, or Bergones, or John, or flash, or John the apostle? If you play the lotto, you pick five numbers out of eighty and then you pick one more number out of the same eighty. The odds of you winning are twenty-nine million to one. So, what are the odds of John calling himself the elder and not something else? And him writing to Gaius, not Alexander or Peter or any other name? How many common names could there be? Two or three hundred? And what are the odds of Gaius taking in the brethren, instead of feeding the poor, or fishing, or teaching? How many different things could he do? Thousands? And this thing be of joy and walking in the truth, instead of something else? And what are the odds he made it so the brethren didn't need to take anything from the Gentiles; say instead of just food from the Gentiles, or from new believers or from Jews or from women, or foreigners? Hundreds? And what are the odds the brethren testified just this thing and not oh, let's say that Paul was a good tent maker, and it was actually heathens, or children, instead of brethren? What are the odds? And the odds that it's Demetrius and not David, and he testified that Mark or Stephen or any other name than Gaius? What are the odds? And that all this testimony and names and places fit the story written by Luke, well now, what are the odds? And John says he's going to visit the region of Gaius instead of say, Rome, or Galatia, or any other area. What would the odds be? The possible different scenarios for every one of these questions are rounded at way more than eighty different choices. There are more than six proofs. If six from eighty is twenty-nine million to one, then I guess by evidence standards, the odds of me being wrong and the scholars being right is not good for the scholars. Look at all the options that John could have added or changed to this letter. Any one of them could bring doubt, but the fact is, there is no doubt. The odds are more than twenty-nine million to one by biblical evidence that the letters were written in AD 57. But as strong as the evidence is for the fifties date, the church refuses to accept it because of the alibi.

Just like in the made-up story, this alibi that scholars believe; that 3rd John was written in the nineties by old man John, is what is needed to convict the Gnostics of the crime of denying Christ in the Bible. In the made-up story, the alibi had to come from someone of authority to make the prosecuting attorney overlook the truth. In this case, we'll say it was his boss, the district attorney, and that is why the alibi in the made-up story has so much weight. The alibi in real life, for the late date of the Epistles comes from high sources also. Scholars, commentators and church leaders enforce this alibi, and the whole world believes it. And amazingly, the most read book in the world is misunderstood.

DEJA VU

Did it Happen two times?

What I find to be even more amazing is that to believe in the story told by scholars, you must believe in Bible deja vu. See you have to believe that all these things that happened in AD 57 to John, happened again in the nineties. Acts, Romans, Corinthians and Galatians tell the story of the fifties. The letter to Gaius is just the result of the accounts told to John, and the things happening at the time of Paul's arrival. If you say the letter John wrote is not of the fifties, but of the nineties, well, all the other stuff still happened. So stories that John heard and lived through thirty to forty years earlier are happening again. You have to believe that more than thirty years later, John heard from the other brethren that the other Gaius was taking in the other brethren above and beyond normal. And the other brethren were taking nothing from the other Gentiles. And the Diotrephes of the story, whom the other Gaius knows isn't taking in the other brethren, just like what was happening in the area that Gaius from the Bible was experiencing. And you have to believe that the other Demetrius, who knows the other Gaius, also has a good testimony of all. And you have to believe that John is going to the other place, from the place that he's at, that is the place that he said he was going to. And you have to believe that. And you have to believe that Luke wrote Acts, and John read Acts, and then wrote a letter that did the book of Acts again. Deja vu. Or maybe I'm not crazy, and you've been lied to. And maybe you need to look past the alibi of, "John wrote his letters in the nineties to combat Gnosticism", and find out just what is going on. The church wants you to believe that John had the most amazing deja vu. But really, if you think about this point, it is totally obvious when John wrote this letter.

When you can see there are no Gnostics in the Bible, and the Epistles of John were written in AD 57, then the Word starts waking up. Your staring right into that fishing net with all the mess, but your still not sure what you're looking at. Your halfway there to seeing what I'm seeing. Two more discernments to go.

4

METAPHORS

The apostles are in the boat and the sea and the wind are tossing them to and fro, till they fear for their lives, and they wake Jesus who is slumbering and cry out!

From: The Author. May my *word* prove worthy.

To: My fellow readers seeking truth. Greetings.

To be enlightened by the true wisdoms of the Word of God, there are four sources one must be able to discern to achieve one's elevated state of knowledge.

With the correct knowledge all things can be known *from the beginning*.

Test all things and hold fast to that which is good. Amen.

In summary, with the first two discernments you had to take something away to see the truth. First you had to remove the fictitious Gnostics that did not exist in first-century Christianity, and second, you had to remove the late dating of the three Epistles of John that was created by scholars. This third discernment is about understanding what you are reading. Knowing that Gnostics did not yet exist, and thus the late date for John's Epistles to combat Gnosticism is untrue, you can now start to see what the writers of the Books were actually saying. What really makes this understanding wake up is the understanding of the metaphors used by the New Testament writers. I hope to start easy and then advance to more complex, and then were gonna rock the boat. I prayed not wanting to go this way myself, rockin' the boat and all, yet my confirmation is to stay in truth, and if this helps to see Jesus, then let's make waves.

My definition of a metaphor is the use of a word or combination of words to describe something that is not its general meaning by dictionary terms or cannot be understood by that word or combination of words without the context of the text. In this book I will refer to many words and phrases as metaphors, and am aware that they on their own would have a different name, yet still by definition are metaphorical. I'm a truck driver, not an English scholar. If it's a simile or synonym, alias, parable or any other contraption that is used to represent something else, in these chapters it will be referred to as a metaphor. My goal with this is to keep it simple and understandable.

In the first pages of this little book, I used several metaphors on purpose just to illustrate how common place they are in how we speak, write, and communicate. I specifically used the word, *word* on purpose to represent several different things. Many years back as an infant Christian I had the opportunity to preach the Word at my local church once a month. I gave this task everything I had and knew that It was anointed by the Spirit of God. That didn't mean I knew what I was preaching. Several of those sermons were taped and as I listened to them just a couple years later, to my surprise, I often missed the mark on many key points. As an example, on one occasion, I preached John 1:1. The point I made from the scripture was that the Word was indeed the Word of God. That's a big point to miss. The Word in this scripture is Jesus. In my zeal to preach about the Bible, and the words of the Bible, I missed the metaphor. When you know the metaphor, you know that John 1:1 says, In the beginning was Jesus, and Jesus was with God, and Jesus was God. Instead I made it say, In the beginning was the Bible, and the Bible was about God, and this is God's word. My point here is that if you miss the metaphor, you can totally miss the meaning.

Now take into consideration that these New Testament books were written almost two thousand years ago in ancient Greek. First, they were translated to Latin and then back to Greek, and from these translations in 1611 to the King James version which is in old English. Now all translations have to match the meaning of the King James and also match the meaning of the ancient Greek manuscripts, and often because of the translation and time issues we miss the meaning of the text. When the cannonizers put the books together, they understood the ancient Greek. They knew exactly what it meant and we just scratch our heads. And scratch our heads is a metaphor for, we don't know what it means.

Ancient Greek writing gave importance, attitude, direction, and character, and meaning to the words with the inflections they attached to the actual word. These would be attached to the word like wings on a bird. The knowledge as to what these inflections mean today is just guesswork. Without knowing their intent, a *we* could be *they* or *if* could be *when*. Those are extreme differences. Ancient Greek scholars only study the root word and then compare it to the work of former scholars.

I once asked a noted internet scholar for an opinion on a block of scripture with metaphors as to the meaning, and all she could give me was the root word phrase. She refused to dabble in the philosophy of what the phrase might actually mean. By this scholastic standard, a metaphor by the New Testament writers could never be recognized unless it was totally deliberate.

I used the word, *word* as a metaphor on several occasions to show how easy even in modern English the meaning can be missed. In the first of this chapter I rewrote the dumb, Gnostic like letter and added one line; May my *word* prove worthy. *Word* in this line is a metaphor for this chapter. In other words, may this chapter prove worthy. In just the first couple pages of this small book, the word, *word* means Jesus, it means the Bible, it means this book, it means the Gospel, and it means word. I didn't go chase them down but I know they are there. I give my word to that. See, there is another one, now *word* also means my promise. Our New Testament writers did the exact same thing. They used words in Greek that after translation and time, scholars have no clue as to what they were talking about, like who is your *brother* in 1ˢᵗ John?

I have a hobby where I do a lot of amateur shooting. In August two years ago, I was preparing for a State match. Concerning my hobby, my wife asked, "So where does Jesus fit in with your shooting?" I quickly answered, "Oh honey, He's right behind me." Later, thinking about my ridiculous answer, I explained that Jesus is not behind me, but He's at my side. I shot the warm-up match on Thursday and then commenced helping to prep for the next day. While moving a table, I slipped a disc in my back. On the way home from the range, I said a little prayer, "Lord, get me through the next two days and I'll deal with the pain later." See, I'd been practicing and preparing for this shoot for a long time, and this amateur cowboy shooting is my favorite thing. No way did I want to miss out on this shoot. Well, I took eight hundred milligrams of ibuprofen when I got home, and eight hundred milligrams more the next morning, and I shot just fine for the next two days. On Sunday there was a shoot-off that I had qualified for, so I shot that. But my back was pretty stiff, even with the ibuprofen. Then later that day I went to work, and by the time I got home, I could hardly walk. For the next several weeks I was taking maximum doses of acetaminophen and Ibuprofen to manage the pain so that I could make it to work and back. Amazingly, I could drive. I would lift my leg with my hand to switch from the throttle to the brake. I have never had so much pain in my life. After work, I would arrive home barley able to move. I would come in the house, go to my bed and get on my knees, say a quick angry prayer, and then lay on the floor in pain waiting for the medicine to start working or to just pass out. I went on like this for a couple months. The pain never ceased. I got to where I was sure I was seeing demons.

Then one day while driving late at night in a place along the road where God has met me before, I turned on the radio and it was Chuck Swindoll, at a time when he's regularly not there. I can't find him in my drive times to this day. And Chuck's talking directly to me. Before I had turned the bend in the road, I had surrendered myself to Jesus, repented of my sins, and was filled with the spirit and healed that night. See, I was now in the right spot. I was behind Jesus, following him. When I say healed, I mean healed. My back was fixed. Whatever was slipped or broke or pinched was now fixed, but there was some residual damage that is still there today. After my injury, to help deal with the pain, a friend recommended a direct therapy TENS device, which is a butterfly-shaped pad that you attach on your back on each side of your spine, and it sends electrical charges into your muscles to relax them. My wife would put this on for me and I would let it run through its cycle of shock rhythms. It was pretty effective at relieving some of the pain. Well, one day after it had been through its cycle, I reached back and peeled the sticky thing off and reapplied it to the lower section right on my tailbone all by myself. I fired it up and was in crazy tweaky pain like I had never felt with this machine before, so I assumed I must have found the actual problem in my back and was dead set to massage it out. I laid there in this shocking pain for about ten minutes before my wife came in to see what was wrong with me. I told her what I had done, and she took a look and instantly told me to turn it off. This machine comes with a warning that says never apply the pads directly to the bone area, and I had the pad right on top of my tailbone. In that ten-minute period, I fried my tailbone. I got a little nerve damage down there. So now I'm better. I'm not as good as I used to be, but I slipped a disc in my back, and ignored that it was hurt for three days, then fried the nerves at my tailbone, and then asked God to heal me through the power of the Holy Spirit, and now I have a thorn in my side. Yep, just like Paul, I have a thorn in my side. Actually, Paul says he has a thorn in the flesh. My thorn in the side is a reminder from God to put Him first. See, I follow Jesus, and sometimes I get this backwards and that's a bad thing. It's shooting season again, and yes, I will play with all my might, but my perspective on my position with the Lord will be with him in front, not equally yoked, or a good leader from behind pressing me on. No, that's garbage. He's right in front and I follow. And I have this pain in my lower backside, yes, a pain in my rear end to remind me of my position.

In my early Christianity, the question as to Paul's thorn in the flesh was presented as unknown and unsolvable. I accepted that answer for a long time, at least until I got to know Paul. See, thorn in the flesh is a metaphor for what is ailing Paul, and over the years it has been presented to mean many things. Pastors say, it could be sickness, or leprosy, or blindness, or a wife, or even memory loss or blaa, bla, bla. Scholars are unsure. I'll say it, scholars have no clue. See it's an obvious metaphor, but for what? "Thorn in my flesh," in modern terms translates to "pain in my backside." So, with biblical evidence what was Paul's thorn? I bet you don't know. Give the thorn a name.

Jesus spoke in Parables. In Mark, Jesus said,

"Hearken; Behold, there went out a sower to sow: and it came to pass, as he sowed, some fell by the wayside, and the fowls of the air came and devoured it up. And some fell on stony ground, where it had not much earth; and immediately it sprang up, because it had no depth of earth: but when the sun was up, it was scorched; and because it had no root, it withered away. And some fell among thorns, and the thorns grew up, and chocked it, and it yielded no fruit. And other fell on good ground and did yield fruit that sprang up and increased; and brought forth, some thirty, and some sixty, and some a hundred." And He said unto them, He that hath ears to hear, let him hear. And when He was alone, they that were about him with the twelve asked of him the parable. And He said unto them, Unto you it is given to know the mystery of the kingdom of God: but unto them that are without, all these things are done in parables, that seeing they may see, and not perceive; and hearing they may hear, and not understand; lest at any time they should be converted, and their sins should be forgiven them. And He said unto them, know ye not this parable? And how then will ye know all the parables? The sower soweth the word. And these are they by the wayside, where the word is sown; but when they have heard, Satan cometh immediately, and taketh away the word that was sown in their hearts. And these are they likewise which are sown on stony ground; who, when they have heard the word, immediately receive it with gladness; and have no root in themselves, and so endure but for a time: afterward, when tribulation or persecution ariseth for the word's sake, immediately they are offended. And these are they which are sown among thorns; such as hear the word, and the cares of this world, and the deceitfulness of riches, and the lusts for other things entering in, choke the word, and it becometh unfruitful. And these are they which are sown on good ground; such as hear the word, and receive it, and bring forth fruit; some thirtyfold, some sixty, and some a hundred." KJV.

This parable is not confusing because Jesus explains to the apostles what it means, giving us the understanding to the metaphors. Furthermore, we have two more accounts of the parable in Matthew and Luke. All three accounts assure us what the metaphors stand for and explain why He was using them, and who it was affecting. In Luke it says,

"And he said, Unto you it is given to know the mysteries of the kingdom of God: but to others in parables; that seeing they may not see and hearing they may not understand. Now the parable is this: The seed is the word of God. Those by the wayside are they that hear; then cometh the devil, and taketh away the word out of their hearts, lest they should believe and be saved. They on the rock are they, which, when they hear, receive the word with joy; and these have no root, which for a while believe, and in time of temptation fall away. And that which fell among thorns are they, which, when they have heard, go forth and are choked with cares and riches and pleasures of this life, and bring no fruit to perfection. But that on the good ground are they, which in an honest and good heart, having heard the word, keep it, and bring forth fruit with patience."

From this we can concur that the seed is a metaphor for the Word of God and the sower is a metaphor for he who spreads the Word. Those by the wayside is a metaphor for the ones who hear, and the birds of the air is a metaphor for the devil that takes it away. Some fell on the rock is a metaphor for those, who when they hear, receive the Word with joy but have no root, and the sun is a metaphor for tribulation, persecution, and temptation, all causing the falling away. Those among thorns is a metaphor for the cares and riches, and pleasures of the world. It says these choke the Word and it doesn't produce fruit. But the ones that fell on good ground is a metaphor for those who, having heard the Word with a noble and good heart, keep it and bear fruit with patience. And fruit is a metaphor for what?

Jesus was speaking in metaphors, and doing it on purpose; so that seeing, they may not see, and hearing they may not understand. In the same story in Matthew, it says,

"And the disciples came and said unto Him, Why speakest thou unto them in parables? He answered and said unto them, Because it is given unto you to know the mysteries of the kingdom of heaven, but to them it is not given. For whosoever hath, to him shall be given, and he shall have more abundance: but whosoever hath not, from him shall be taken away even that he hath."

So I ask, "what will be given and taken away?" Jesus said, the understanding of the mysteries of heaven. And that *mystery of heaven* is a metaphor for Jesus is the Son of God. Then He said,

"Therefore speak I to them in parables: because they seeing see not; and hearing they hear not, neither do they understand. And in them is fulfilled the prophesy of Isaiah, which saith, By hearing ye shall hear, and shall not understand; and seeing ye shall see, and shall not perceive. For the people's heart is waxed gross, and their ears are dull of hearing, and their eyes they have closed; lest at any time they should see with their eyes, and hear with their ears, and should understand with their heart, and should be converted, and I should heal them. But blessed are your eyes, for they see: and your ears, for they hear. For verily I say unto you, that many prophets and righteous men have desired to see those things which ye see, and have not seen them; and hear those things which ye hear, and have not heard them."

In three separate accounts, Jesus says his message is not to be understood by them. Who are them? *Them* is a metaphor for the Pharisees, Sadducees, and Scribes. Them are right there listening to him on the wayside. They see the miracles and don't believe, and they hear the words and don't understand.

Jesus was the teacher and He taught in metaphors to confuse the wise, and He gave His followers the key by explaining this parable. He said in Mark, if you don't understand this parable, how can you understand any of the parables? Peter and John were students of this teaching.

I said I would start easy and move to a little more difficult, so from here let's go to the metaphors of Peter. His two Epistles take about thirty minutes to read and are straight forward and to the point, yet because of time, translation, and a handful of metaphors, they can be hard to understand. I will cover four metaphors. There are many more, but with these four, the obvious metaphors just become part of the story. Peter starts his first Epistle by addressing it, "To the strangers scattered throughout Pontus, Galatia, Cappadocia, Asia, and Bithynia, Elect…". KJV. By my truck driver standards, *strangers* is a metaphor. When the Babylonians sacked Israel several hundred years earlier, the twelve tribes were dispersed from their land and scattered to all the regions, and their land was given to foreigners, thus making them the *strangers*. Modern Bibles use the word exiles, pilgrims of the dispersion, foreigners and aliens instead of *strangers*. They are all different metaphors for the scattered Jews in those regions. *Elect* is a metaphor for those that follow Jesus Christ. They are His chosen. Peter is writing to the Christian Jews of these regions. Those metaphors are not hard to understand, and neither is the next, the word *tabernacle*. This is a metaphor used in 2nd Peter to describe his mortal body. So, where is Peter? In the end of 1st Peter he says, "The church that is in Babylon, elect together with you, saluteth you; and so doth Markus my son". KJV. Now this can be a doozie. I will tell you right now that most scholars have no idea where Peter is at. There are three good choices and they are, Jerusalem, Rome, or Babylon. Take a pick. What? You're not sure. Here, let me help you be sure.

In the reign of King Hezekiah, the Babylonian King Sennerichib sent his army and sacked Israel but not Judea, as King Hezekiah was a King with Gods favor. The tribes were dispersed all over the land at this time. Several hundred years later in the time of the prophet Jeremiah, Judea got sacked by the Babylonian King Nebuchadnezzar, and the reigning Jewish king along with all the jewels of the temple and everything else of value were gobbled up and taken to Babylon. Thus, Babylon is a place, but Peter is not there. Biblical proof says so. I'll show you. *Babylon* is a metaphor, so the question is what does the metaphor stand for?

I heard commentary one time when a radio pastor who was not sure of the location described by Peter said that he asked a Jewish scholar of the Bible, and that scholars answer was adamant and point of fact, that any Jew reading this scripture would without doubt know that Peter was in Jerusalem. At that time Jerusalem would have been compared to Babylon because of the Roman occupation. I thought that an excellent answer, but then knowing that Babylon is a metaphor and wanting to test this answer with biblical proof, I did, and well, it did not pass the test. Peter is not in Jerusalem. So how do I know Peter is in Rome? First, what does the metaphor stand for? Babylon was a place of captivity, and Babylon was the home of the enemy. Thus, to be in the metaphoric Babylon, Peter must be in Rome. Second, in 1st Peter he refers to himself, as an apostle, and in 2nd Peter, he refers to himself as a bondservant and an apostle. A bondservant suggests that he is a prisoner for Christ. Third, Peter says he is about to fulfill the promises of Christ. Jesus said to Peter in the last chapter of John that he would be crucified. That's what happens to prisoners in Rome. See, Peter's crime is the same as Paul's, and Paul was sent to Rome. Fourth, and I love this one, Peter's letters were written by Sylvanus. We know that Sylvanus was in Rome with Paul. Fifth, Peter ends with greetings from his son Mark, and we know that in Paul's letters to Timothy, he said to bring Mark to Rome. Sixth, Peter says that Paul's writings are hard to understand, meaning he had access to the writings being delivered by Sylvanus to the Galatians. Seventh, Peter's letters were delivered to the Jews among the Galatians by the same messenger. And that is Biblical evidence that Peter is in Rome, and it is evidence to show when he was there. Go ahead and tell me you knew that.

By understanding that a word is a metaphor and then using biblical information, you can discern what it stands for. With this information and the realization that scholars don't know, the Bible will start to come alive. What is the *thorn* in Paul's flesh? Who is the great *Theopolis*? Who is your *brother* in 1st John? The answers are there, but first, let's look at the key to 1st John. The key to understanding the metaphors in 1st John is the 2nd Epistle of John. Jesus was the teacher, and I like to refer to Paul as the king of metaphors, and he wasn't even present for Jesus' teachings, but I call John the magic man. Let me show you why.

I present to you,

The Second Epistle of John

> The Elder, unto the elect lady and her children, whom I love in truth; and not I only, but also all they who have known the truth; for the truth's sake, which dwelleth in us, and shall be with us forever. Grace be with you, mercy, and peace from God the Father, and from the Lord Jesus Christ, the Son of the Father, in truth and love.
>
> I rejoiced greatly that I found of thy children walking in truth, as we have received a commandment from the Father. And now I beseech thee, lady, not as though I wrote a new commandment unto thee, but that which we had from the beginning, that we love one another. And this is love, that we walk after his Commandments. This is the commandment, that,

as ye have heard from the beginning, ye should walk in it.

For many deceivers are entered into the world, who confess not that Jesus Christ is come in the flesh. This is a deceiver and an antichrist. Look to yourselves, that we lose not those things which we have wrought, but that we receive a full reward. Whosoever transgresseth, and abideth not in the doctrine of Christ, hath not God. He that abideth in the doctrine of Christ, he hath both the Father and the Son. If there come any unto you, and bring not this doctrine, receive him not into your house, neither bid him Godspeed: for he that biddeth him Godspeed is a partaker of his evil deeds.

Having many things to write unto you, I would not write with paper and ink; but I trust to come unto you, and speak face to face, that our joy may be full.

The children of thy elect sister greet thee. Amen. KJV.

Here's a letter to some lady and her children, and John says he rejoiced to see them walking in the commandment of the Father and pleads that we love one another. Many deceivers don't confess Jesus Christ as coming in the flesh. These transgressors don't abide to the doctrine of Christ, and don't have God. If anyone comes to you and does not have this doctrine don't let them in your house, and don't greet them. Those who wish him well shares in his evil deeds. Hope to see you soon. How does this make John the magic man? Once you see his metaphors and you understand them, then the letters start to come alive with more meaning, and you can see who your *brother* is in 1st John. It's like magic because till now you don't know it's even there.

Why is this simple letter in the Bible? It's not hard to understand, and it says what it says. Don't let into your house those who deny that Jesus was born God among us. So why is that in the Bible? It's a key to the understanding of 1st John. Just like the information in 3rd John dates the letter to the time of Paul's return from his third missionary journey, and puts these Epistles in AD 57, the 2nd Epistle of John along with clues from the 3rd Epistle give us the keys to the metaphors in 1st John. I explained earlier in this chapter how I used the word *word* incorrectly by thinking it to mean the word of God when it truly meant Jesus Christ. John has done the same thing as he did with the word *word* with several words in these letters, and when you understand that they are metaphors the letter says a different thing. John has done the same thing with the word, *truth*. *Truth* is a metaphor for fellowship with Jesus Christ.

A count of metaphors, (i.e. words meaning something else) in this small letter; there are approximately seventeen.

1. Lady-church
2. Her-the church's
3. Children-members
4. Truth-fellowship with Jesus Christ
5. Truth-fellowship with Jesus Christ
6. Truth-fellowship with Jesus Christ
7. Your children-members of you church
8. Walking-practicing
9. Truth-fellowship with Jesus Christ
10. Lady-church
11. From the beginning-Jesus Christ
12. From the beginning-Jesus Christ
13. Coming in the flesh-God born amongst us
14. Full reward-eternal life
15. House-church
16. Children-members
17. Sister-my church

So, the first sentence would look like this. "To the elect church and its members whom I love in our fellowship with Jesus Christ, and not only I but also all those who have the same fellowship in Him, because of the fellowship of Jesus Christ which abides in us and will be with us forever. Grace, mercy, and peace will be with you from God the Father and from the Lord Jesus Christ, the Son of the Father, in truth and love."

Many a Pharisee pastor would have to wail and tear his robe at the last written sentence because he would be sure that it must be blaspheme. Remember why Jesus spoke in parables? Jesus used metaphors to confound the wise, and His pupil uses metaphors to protect the flock from those same wise. In two sentences John used the word *truth* five times, and only one of them being truth by dictionary terms.

Because the format of the letter is just like that of 3rd John, and from the content of 3rd John we know that there are contentions in the church, and the fact that Paul is in chains and would soon to be heading to Rome, John had a need to write this letter in a manner that no specific entity could be accused of placing Jesus before Caesar and thus be put before the Romans. The letter was meant to look like a letter to a lady, not a church, thus giving it no strength as evidence against this particular church.

With clues from 1st and 3rd John, and 1st Peter, these metaphors become obviously correct. In 3rd John, he says to Gaius, "For I rejoiced greatly, when the brethren came and testified of the truth that is in thee, even as thou walkest in the truth. I have no greater joy than to hear that my children walk in truth." KJV. So Gaius is that believer walking in fellowship with Christ. John is not Gaius's daddy. 1st John starts, "That which was *from the beginning*, which we have heard, which we have seen with our eyes, which we have looked upon, and our hands have handled, of the Word of life;". KJV (Italics added). *From the beginning*, in that sentence, is a metaphor for Jesus Christ, which we have heard and seen, and hung out with and touched. And 1st Peter says, "The church that is at Babylon, elected together with you, saluteth you." KJV. Most all modern versions of this sentence start with the word *she* and that *she* is the church of Rome. So we can concur from other references in the same period of time, that the metaphors are accurate. And without 2nd John to confirm the metaphors, a lot of 1st John cannot be seen and understood by todays standard of translation.

John wrote this short note of 2nd John to a church to be delivered by the traveling companions of Paul on their return trip. It says, "Don't let those that say Jesus is not born God into your church, and I hope to see you soon." It is easy to completely understand the letters when you are aware of the metaphors. *Lady, children, sister* and *home* are all metaphors for the church and its members, while *truth,* and *from the beginning,* and *coming in the flesh* are metaphors for Jesus Christ. When you can see the metaphors and know that *truth* is fellowship with Jesus Christ, and *from the beginning* is Jesus Christ, and *came in the flesh* is Jesus born the Christ among us, then you are starting to understand the third discernment. Your *brother* in 1st John is a metaphor. John wrote in metaphors to confuse those that were persecuting the church. For those that received this letter, they understood completely what John was conveying in this note. Scholars still miss the metaphors because they never read the story of the Bible. All of these metaphors for Jesus are thoroughly explained in John's writings. He is not copying someone else's metaphors. He is using his own. On the first page of 1st John, he writes, that truly our fellowship is with the Father and Jesus Christ, so *truth* is fellowship with Jesus Christ. There are not optional answers to what John might have been saying when you know John's writings.

Let's play a little devil's advocate and assume that I'm wrong. And truth just means truth (as in true), and there's no magic here. Paraphrased, this letter says, "To the lady and her children, whom I love in truth, and not only I, but those who know the truth, because of the truth that we know and will know forever." John loves this lady and her children, and that is the truth, and everyone that knows the truth also loves them, because of the truth that they know is forever? What is the truth? If it is not Jesus then is it love or is it just mystical. That sounds like Gnosticism. Not like it's combating Gnosticism, but like it's the foundation for *The Gospel of Truth* from the 2nd century. In the fourth chapter of The *Gospel of Truth* by Valentinus, it says that Jesus enlightened them and gave a path to truth, and that's what he taught. It appears that *The Gospel of Truth* stems from the word *truth* in Johns Epistles. Valentinus, apparently could not see the metaphors. When you cannot see the magic, it's easy to get lost, and truth becomes debatable to a point of being unknown. Oh, that's heavy, but it becomes obvious that the Epistles of John are the seed that rooted *The Gospel of truth* in the second century due to Valentinus' lack of understanding of John's metaphors. Therefore, to support the phrasing of truth as word correct, and the meaning of *truth* to just true, makes John the elder into John the Gnostic. This is why your pastor preaches the love letter. John truly loves the lady and everybody that knows that John loves the lady also loves the lady, because truth is love. This is the modern church doctrine, and this is as wrong as when I preached and made the *Word* referring to Jesus in John 1:1 say the *Word* is the Bible. If you flip your Bible back one page to the last sentences of 1st John, it says (paraphrased) that we know that Jesus has come and given us the understanding so that we know Jesus who is *true*. And it says, we are in Jesus who is *true*, that Jesus is the *true* God and eternal life. Then two lines later we get confused in 2nd John and think truth is love? It's just stupid. John was consistent in his message.

John tells us exactly what the truth is. Let me show you how he sews. Yes, like a needle and thread; he is a quilter. Let's look at some of his patterns. In the Gospel of John, he records the metaphors that Jesus used to identify Himself followed by action. Jesus said, "I am the bread of life." Then He said, "He that cometh to Me shall never hunger; and he that believeth on Me shall never thirst." Jesus said,

"I am the light of the world." Then He said, "He who followeth Me shall not walk in darkness, but shall have the light of life." Jesus said, "I am the door." Then He said, "By Me if any man enters in, he shall be saved, and shall go in and out, and find pasture." Jesus said, "I am the good shepherd;", then He said, "And I know my sheep, and am known of mine." Jesus said, "I am the resurrection and the life." Then He said, "He who believeth in Me, though he were dead, yet, shall he live. Jesus said, "I am the way, the truth, and the life." Then He said, "No man cometh unto the father but by me." Jesus said, "I am the vine, ye are the branches." Then He said, "He who abideth in me, and I in him, the same bringeth forth much fruit: for without me ye can do nothing." Do you see the pattern? Those are Bible quotes from the Book of John, word for word KJV, nothing added and nothing taken away except for the, *then he said.*

In the Book of Genesis, Moses started with, "In the beginning God created the heaven and the earth." Then he said, "And the earth was without form, and void; and darkness was upon the face of the deep. And the Spirit of God moved upon the face of the waters. And God said, let there be light: and there was light." KJV. In the book, the Gospel according to John, John started with, "In the beginning was the Word, and the Word was with God, and the Word was God." Then He said, "The same was in the beginning with God. All things were made by him; and without him was not anything made that was made. In him was life; and the life was the light of men." KJV. In the book, The First Epistle of John, John started with, "That which was from the beginning, which we have heard, which we have seen with our eyes, which we have looked upon, and our hands have handled, of the Word of life;" then he said, "For the life was manifested, and we have seen it, and bear witness, and show unto you that eternal life, which was with the Father, and was manifested unto us; that which we have seen and heard declare we unto you, that ye also may have fellowship with us: and *truly* our fellowship is with the Father, and with His Son Jesus Christ." KJV. In the book, The Second Epistle of John, John started with, "The elder unto the elect lady and her children, whom I love in truth; and not I only, but also all they that have known the truth; for the truth's sake, which dwelleth in us, and shall be with us forever." KJV. Do you see the quilters pattern?

Moses wrote, In the beginning God created, and then God said, let there be light. Then John wrote, In the beginning was the Word, that was with God. Jesus was there in the beginning and He was the light of Men. Then John wrote, that which was from the beginning who was with us concerning the word of life, we declare, and truly our fellowship is with the Father and His Son Jesus Christ. Then John wrote to the lady and her children whom I love in truth. Moses said, God created light, and John wrote the Word is the light of man, then he wrote that the Word from the beginning is truly, I repeat truly, who we are in fellowship with, and then he writes, I love you in truth. In this pattern the Word is Jesus, *from the beginning* is Jesus, and *truth* is Jesus. This is an awesome pattern and it mimics the words of Jesus.

I want to confirm that *truth* in The Second Epistle of John is Jesus Christ. Here is another pattern of the quilter magic man. In the 1st Epistle John writes, "and truly our fellowship is with the Father, and with his Son Jesus Christ". Then three sentences down he writes, "If we say that we have fellowship with Him, and walk in darkness, we lie, and do not the truth:" Just a little further into the letter John writes, "He that saith, I know him, and keepeth not his commandments, is a liar, and the truth is not in him. But whoso keepeth his word, in him verily is the love of God perfected:" And further down John writes, "I have not written unto you because ye know not the truth, but because ye know it, and that no lie is of the truth." And just a little further in the letter, John writes, "But the anointing which ye have received from him abideth in you, and ye need not that any man teach you: but as the same anointing teacheth you of all things, and is true, and is no lie, and even as it hath taught you, ye shall abide in him." Then later in the letter, John writes, "We are of God: he that knoweth God heareth us; he that is not of God heareth not us. Hereby know we the spirit of <u>truth,</u> and the spirit of error." John finishes this letter with, "And we know that the Son of God is come, and hath given us an understanding, that we may know him that is <u>true</u>, and we are in him that is <u>true</u>, even in his Son Jesus Christ. This is the <u>true</u> God and eternal life." That is the pattern of truth in the 1st Epistle of John, KJV (underline added). From his other patterns we know they carry from book to book, so what is the truth?

John said, *truth* is our fellowship with the Father and the Son. You cannot walk in darkness and have fellowship; you cannot break the commandments of Jesus and have fellowship, but keep His words and the love of God is perfected in this fellowship. There is no lie in this relationship. The anointing you have received confirms this and brings you into fellowship. Those who are in fellowship with God hear us, and those who are not in fellowship do not. By this we know that we follow Jesus and not the world. The Son of God has come and has given us understanding, that we may know God who is true; and we are in God who is true, in Gods Son, Jesus Christ. This is the true God and eternal life. What is *truth*? The quilter says truth is a relationship with Jesus Christ. Amen.

On a personal note, at this point in this writing, while at work on the road after writing the previous section and contemplating my direction, while talking with God, I had a moment where I spontaneously uttered outload, by no thought of my own, a foreign noise. I laughed, and said out loud to myself, what was that? I then realized, I had just spoke in tongues, and I don't speak in tongues, ever. I was instantly shown a string I had not seen before, and then got slammed with the Holy Spirit. Overwhelmed! I just held on to the wheel and let it flow. What is fruit?

So, now when reading the 2nd Epistle of John, there should be no doubt as to what the metaphor of *truth* is. We know the *elect lady* is a church because Jesus referred to Himself as the Bridegroom, and the Books say that the church is the bride, making the church a she, and elect making it the ones chosen, assures us that John is writing to a church. The salutation in this 2nd Epistle confirms this. The *children* are the church members. John writes children using the same pattern as in The Gospel of John, where he says that when you accept Jesus you become a child of God. *From the beginning* is described in the opening of 1st John, and with these everything else falls into place. It is a letter written to a church with the message of fellowship with Jesus and love for one another, and then there is one more metaphor. "For many deceivers are entered into the world, who confess not that Jesus Christ is *come in the flesh*. This is a deceiver and an antichrist." KJV (italics added).

This is the metaphor that has more than likely helped to create the false doctrines of the Gnostics in the 2nd century and leads scholars to believe John was fighting Gnosticism. To a scholar, Jesus not coming in the flesh says that John was fighting against Gnostics. Scholars never read the book with the understanding that *came in the flesh*, is a metaphor. Yeah, it's a prepositional phrase, but by my truck driver simplicity standards, it's a metaphorical prepositional phrase. It means Jesus is God in the form of man. *Came in the flesh* equals God born among us. Follow the quilters pattern. On the first page of the Gospel of John, he wrote, "And the Word was made flesh, and dwelt among us, and we beheld his glory, the glory as of the only begotten of the Father, full of grace and truth." KJV. That says Jesus Christ was born flesh and dwelt among us. In 1st John, he writes, "Who is a liar but he that denieth that Jesus is the Christ? He is antichrist that denieth the Father and the Son. Whosoever denieth the Son, the same have not the Father: but he that acknowledgeth the Son hath the Father also." KJV. And later in the letter John writes, "Hereby know ye the spirit of God: Every spirit that confesseth that Jesus Christ is come in the flesh is of God: and every spirit that confesseth not that Jesus Christ is come in the flesh is not of God:" KJV. John says anyone who denies that Jesus was born the Son of God is not of us and don't let them in your church. In the Gospel of John, Jesus said to the quarreling Jews at the synagogue in Capernaum, "Verily, verily, I say unto you, except ye eat the flesh of the Son of man, and drink His blood, ye have no life in you." KJV. They had no idea what He was saying. They are those on the wayside. Jesus started this conversation with, "I am the bread of life: he that cometh to me shall never hunger; and he that believeth on me shall never thirst." Thus, coming equals eating, and believing equals drinking, and flesh equals Christ. And all through the Gospels, the Pharisees, the Sadducees, and the Scribes refused to accept Jesus as the Christ, as the Son of God, as coming in the flesh. It doesn't say Jesus came in the flesh, it says Jesus **Christ** came in the flesh. Jesus was born the Son of God. There are no Gnostics in the Bible, only those from the wayside who could not see or understand. Can you see the metaphor? Can you see the pattern? At this saying of Jesus, many stopped following because it was too hard. So I ask, where do you stand? The doctrine of scholars, or biblical truth?

Jesus, like everyone else, had no last name. You were the son of somebody, or from a place, or known by your occupation, or by your tribe. Thus, Jesus of Nazareth, or Jesus the son of the carpenter, Jesus the son of Joseph, Jesus from the tribe of Judah, or even Jesus the prophet. See, The Pharisees, Sadducees, and Scribes all knew that Jesus. He came in the flesh. He was among them. They hung Him on a cross. What they never accepted was Jesus the Christ, the Son of God, that the King of the world was amongst them. They were from the wayside and could not comprehend and denied that God in the flesh was among us. Flesh equals Jesus Christ born God among us.

Is the boat rockin' a little? See the magic. Every metaphor John used is described in his first two books, and has an explanation word for word, but scholars don't see it. Maybe you don't see it. Can only the children see it? Every point I used to explain the 2nd Epistle of John came from the writings of John. Everything outside the letters of John are just more confirmation. Jesus said, to fulfill the prophesy of Isaiah, and I'm paraphrasing, So, that those who see cannot see, and those who hear will not understand. I pray, "Thank you Lord for not allowing me to be a scholar."

What else do we know about this letter? Where is it going, and who are the children? Evidence is not as strong, but there is some. Probably more I don't see yet, and still more outside the Bible. I tell my wife, honey, when your ninety, which is some long way still, she's fifty-six, I'll come up and smack you on the knee while your resting in your easy chair, and say, honey, I finally figured it out! She'll smile and say, that's nice, good work honey, and then go on with her nap. She's got Jesus, and these are just particulars to her, but to me it's fascinating. It's truth. From the 3rd Epistle we know the time frame, and from Acts we know who was traveling with Paul that would have met John. They were Corinthians, Philippians, and Ephesians. From the 3rd Epistle and Acts we know that Gaius is a Philippian. And from 1st Corinthians and Romans we know that he would be aware of the activities in these churches. We know from Paul's first letter to the Corinthians that they had issues, and the biggest one being the question of Jesus being the Son of God who had risen from the dead, or did you miss that because of the metaphors. I call John the magic man of metaphors, but I refer to Paul as the king. I will show you why shortly, but you may need to grab a life jacket.

Doctrinal Preservation

I had just finished the outline for chapter four on Saturday, so I said to my wife, "let's go to a local church this Sunday". She readily agreed because the alternative is no church. We moved forty miles away over a month ago and haven't been to church since. I've got lots of excuses. She asks, where do you want to go? I say a specific big church that we have both attended in the past before we met, but have never been to together. She was reluctant with the choice, but agreed thinking the worship would be wonderful. I wanted to go there because I went there before and it was easy to slip in and slip out. So we had a plan. All we had to do was confirm the start time.

Jess searched on her phone and found everything and anything about this church except the start time, so I googled it on the internet. Easy enough, it starts at nine thirty and eleven, and then I got excited because the whole computer screen read 1st John. Is the Lord leading me to like-minded believers? My enthusiasm went to skepticism really fast. This was the eighth sermon from 1st John, with the title of the series being "The Genuine Jesus." So far in the first seven sermons, the Pastor has made it to verse ten. Does he see what I see? I'm not feeling good about it, so I opened his first message from seven weeks back, which was his introduction to the series. Within fifteen minutes he had made the most important points of 1st John; that he is ninety plus years old and the Gnostics are infiltrating the church. That's all I could take. This means in seven messages, at forty-five minutes a message, he has already spent way over three hundred minutes to incorrectly describe three minutes of scripture. In that five hours of time, you could read this book, the Epistles of John, and the last of Acts. We didn't make it to church, but we got motivated.

I promise you that this Pastor has no idea who your brother is in 1st John. My wife and I know the Lord showed us this church for a reason. It's a wonderful church, preaching a scholarly accepted doctrine, none the less, it is hard for me to go to church right now. Even though every Pastor is truly doing the work of God, the things I hear preached are distorted every time, and I find it confusing and my confusion does not make it easy for my wife. When I was looking for like-minded people on the internet a couple years ago, my wife showed me Chuck Smith, the founder of Calvary Chapel. I love Calvary because they are Bible-based. She shows me a video where Chuck is explaining how he started. I'm going from memory, but basically, he says, for the first whole year he preached from 1st John. Ok, but he has no clue who your brother is in 1st John. I picture fifty-two sermons with ninety-year-old John fighting Gnostics. He is not alone. Look on the internet. There are a good twenty preachers ready to share 1st John, and within ten minutes they all explain he's ninety years old and combating Gnosticism. At the same time I watched Chuck Smith, I got excited because there was a recent new book out on the Epistles of John, so I watched for a couple minutes. This scholar said he studied the best fifty scholars on the Epistles of John and came up with what must be the most accurate story of the books. He has no clue who your brother is in 1st John. Ask any Pastor what 1st John is about and you know they're going to say? The exact same thing! You know why? It's doctrine. It's what every seminary student in every school of religion is taught. Ironically, the philosophy protecting this incorrect doctrine is based from a verse in 2nd John. "If there come any unto you, and bring not this doctrine, receive him not into your house..." KJV.

2nd John is referred to as a book, but is nothing more than a very short letter, and by todays terms, we would call it a quick note. It doesn't cover half a page. In the 2nd Epistle, John says that anyone coming and preaching a different doctrine than this, don't let them in your church. This doctrine then meant that Jesus Christ came in the flesh, and thus, Jesus was born God amongst us. Any other doctrine in the case of Johns letter, would deny that Jesus was born the Christ and the Son of God, and would be that doctrine of the Sadducees, and would be the same doctrine that Paul was fighting against that says the dead don't rise, and Jesus was not the Christ and is dead. The truth in this short note can't be seen today because of the doctrine of our predecessors. The doctrine that says John was battling Gnostics at the end of the 1st century. Thus, the people that won't change doctrine, even if it's in error, because of the effects it could have on Christianity are the ones that already changed it, and are teaching a doctrine different than the doctrine of the Bible. The only standing evidence for their doctrine is nothing. That's right. There is no evidence to prove that John wrote the Epistles in AD 90 and no evidence to prove Gnostics are in the Bible! Show any evidence for Gnostics in the Bible, and I assure you that they are the Pharisees, Sadducees, and Scribes. Bible evidence shows it every time. Show evidence outside the Bible, and every time, it will be from a later era, and easily proven false. There is no evidence.

Show any evidence for John's books being written in AD 90, and I will assure you, by Bible evidence, that it's not evidence at all. Show the evidence outside the Bible, and upon close scrutiny, you will see that it is not evidence. All that is there is scholarly opinion based on St. Irenaeus and circumstance that is passed as doctrine. Why must this doctrine stand? The church will tell you that it's the foundation of Christ, and therefore, it cannot change. I tell you that the Bible is the foundation of Christ, and the foundation of religion is what killed Him at the first coming. When the church through ignorance, established a doctrine of a battle against Gnosticism, they covered up and came close to erasing the simple doctrine of Christ.

I will show you who Paul is battling in 1st Corinthians. A couple years ago, I was studying in 1st Corinthians and working to understand a block of scripture. I had what I thought was a good understanding of what Paul was saying, but still, some verses were evading me as to the connection with the rest of the text. Therefore, when my Pastor at that time, was going verse by verse through the book of 1st Corinthians, I was quite excited: So much that I sat and wrote a letter explaining my belief in the meaning of the text, and how I got to that conclusion. Then I hand delivered the letter. Knowing we were still weeks away from this specific block of scripture, and never hearing a word on my letter, I wrote a second letter with more pertinent information on this area of scripture. As I was going through the letter, I started seeing patterns in Paul's writing. I hand delivered this one also and was told by my busy pastor that he would get around to looking at my letters in the near future. Well, several more weeks passed, and finally we were at that place in the book, the pinnacle of Paul's letter, and my pastor, who goes verse by verse through the Bible, skipped a couple verses, and made some weird and awkward comments to this block of scripture, and then read on. To say the least, I was totally frustrated and angry. Not only did he never acknowledge my opinions to me, but he never shared his own opinions for this section of scripture. I commenced to writing a third letter that was seething in indignation. Yes, I was irritated that after two letters citing biblical evidence, my pastor still didn't get it. So I wrote it out verse by verse with meaning, and now because of the urgency and irritation on this subject, just like that of Paul, I suddenly didn't kind of know what Paul was writing, but I understood the block of scripture completely. Paul was irritated and frustrated when he wrote this part of the letter. In my irritation, I seen his. This time I sent the letter email and pastor got back to me in just a day. He apologized via email, for never reading my two letters, and stated, he never seen a better answer for the block of scripture. So what did Paul write?

"Else what shall they do which are baptized for the dead, if the dead rise not at all? Why are they then baptized for the dead? And why do we stand in jeopardy every hour? I protest by your rejoicing which I have in Christ Jesus our Lord, I die daily. If after the manner of men I have fought with beasts of Ephesus, what advantageth it me, if the dead rise not? Let us eat and drink; for tomorrow we die. Be not deceived: evil communications corrupt good manners. Awake to righteousness, and sin not; for some have not the knowledge of God. I speak this to your shame." KJV, and oh, I miss my NKJV.

This block of scripture is all metaphor, but before I share it, I want to set the mind frame of Paul. You and your six-year-old son, little Johnny, go to the next-door neighbors to visit and see their new puppy. (Yes, I'm inserting a little Johnny story. There's ridiculous humor in it to me.) Little Suzie, who is four, is sitting on the back porch, all dressed up, with a big smile and pony tails in her hair, and she's just beaming with joy over the new puppy nestled in her lap. As you are conversing with your neighbor, you watch as little Johnny walks up to sweet little Suzie and her new puppy, expecting a pleasant reaction from your son. As Johnny reaches out toward the puppy, it flinches in surprise of the strange hand and yelps like sometimes puppies do when they're startled. At this, Johnny flinches back startled himself, and then reaches out and smacks the puppy on the nose. This totally frightens little Suzie, and before you can cover the distance to the porch, little Johnny has grabbed little Suzie by the pony tail and then slaps Suzie on the nose. As a loving parent, how do you respond? Personally, my child would be flying through the air as I'm gripping him with one hand and trying to flip him in the correct position for a one shot, open air butt whopping, as I'm heading to the front door, apologizing and navigating myself back home, where little Johnny is going to be sitting in a corner fearing for his life, while I calm down and contemplate how to explain to a six-year-old what you never, never, ever do. Sure, I go overboard, and am aware, that as a parent I failed both in patience and child rearing, and I have to make my son understand what is right and what is wrong. The point I need to make to you, is how, in love, do you explain this to your child, and insure that it does not happen again. My explanation looks something like this. "You never, ever hit girls! You never pull hair, you never push or fight with girls ever! Do you understand? Please repeat what I said, so I know you understand". All this is said with authority and love, and then hugs and promises, and an apology to little Suzie and her parents from both of us, and more hugs I hope.

Compare your personal reaction with your little Johnny to mine, and then think, what was Paul thinking? Some of Paul's children were thinking the dead don't rise. His statement has anger, sarcasm, correction, and love.

Now we need a simple understanding of a couple metaphor standards in the Epistles. Start with *dead*. In the New Testament writings *dead* does not hardly ever mean dead, and *dead* most of the time means being unsaved; as not having a relationship with Jesus Christ. In the same sense, followers of Jesus that have died, are said to be *asleep*. They will be awakened and risen at His coming.

In this last part of Paul's letter to the Corinthians, after giving correction advice on everything they asked, he has got to the pinnacle point of the letter. It happens to be the same most important point he makes in every letter; that Jesus rose from the dead and is the Son of God. He writes, "For I delivered unto you first of all that which I also received, how that Christ died for our sins according to the scriptures; and that he was buried, and that he rose again the third day according to the scriptures." KJV. Then a little further on he gets to the problem they're having in Corinth. He writes, "Now if Christ be preached that he rose from the dead, how say some among you that there is no resurrection of the dead?" KJV. That would be from the Sadducees. They don't believe in life after death or angels. That is their doctrine, and just as Christians believe they must share the doctrine of Christ, the Sadducees were spreading their doctrine. How do I know it's the Sadducees? Everything Paul writes says so, and the book of Acts says so, and the metaphors say so. This line, "Let us eat and drink; for tomorrow we die;" KJV is a quote from Isaiah 22:13. It is a prophesy of the tumbling of Israel and Judea by King Nebuchadnezzar and the Babylonians, that happened several hundred years earlier. It says that it's a time when all is lost and there is no more worshiping God, so let us eat and drink for tomorrow we die. This is the verse the Sadducees use in their fine and proper well-trained speaking for the belief that the dead do not rise. The Corinthians have asked Paul what does it mean? After stating the question, Paul explains that if Christ is not risen from the dead, everything we preach and believe is futile and lost. Then he says, paraphrased, but Christ has risen, and is the first fruits for those who have fallen asleep, which are the ones who died believing in Jesus, and then goes on putting things in order with Christ conquering the world; making all things subject to him. And then there is this block of scripture. It's a rant on the Sadducees, a correction to the Corinthians, and a big, what are we here for if Jesus did not rise!

I wrote early on that everything written in the Bible has to match all the early translations, and the earliest Greek versions, and deal with time and language changes, and that all the inflections have been neutered. This is one of those places that doesn't fare well. I change nor alter not a single word of Greek, and I tell you my early Bible translators did not understand what Paul was saying because of metaphors. I mentioned earlier that I asked a noted Greek scholar about a block of scripture. This is that scripture. She refused to step outside what scholars have already written in their lexicons and concordances and could not dabble in philosophy. I'm not going to dabble in philosophy either. I'm going to tell you what it says. Dynamic paraphrased translation.

> "Otherwise, why do we baptize the unsaved, if Jesus did not rise? Why are we baptizing the unsaved? Because Jesus rose, that's why! And why do we face persecution for this belief every day? Because Jesus rose, that's why! Why do I brag of your relationship with Jesus Christ to the point of sin? Because Jesus rose! Why am I fighting with the Jews of Ephesus? What advantage is it to me? It's nothing unless Jesus rose! If the dead do not rise, as the Sadducees say; "Let's eat and drink, for tomorrow we die". Do not be deceived: "Evil company destroys good practices". Awake to righteousness, and do not sin; for some do not have the knowledge of God. I write this to your shame."

I told you, Paul is the King of metaphors. *Dead* is unsaved, then *dead* is Jesus, then *dead* is unsaved, then *jeopardy* is persecutions, then *die* is sin, then *beasts* is Ephesian Sadducees, and then a quote from Isaiah, for a metaphorical paragraph that no one understands. But now you do. When you understand that in the story line Paul has already confirmed that Christ has risen, and is God, and then asks four rhetorical, sarcastic, and metaphorical questions to make his point, then you understand what Paul is writing.

If you think Paul was maybe saying something else other than Jesus rose from the dead, then why is it the main course in all his writings, and the very reason he is in chains in Rome, and his boat tipped over on the way there. I had to throw that in. Paul started 1st Corinthians writing about baptism in Christ, and finished with that same baptism, and everything makes sense.

What was the thorn in Paul's flesh? No dabble. His name was Alexander the coppersmith. He was a Sadducee and an Ephesian, and he was the wild beast Paul had to deal with. Paul said that he prayed three times to have this *thorn* depart from him. Paul had exiled him from the Church of Ephesus and referred to him as the messenger of Satan. Paul fought with him in Ephesus to the point of causing riots in the coliseum. Paul was thrown out of the Temple in Jerusalem by Alexander, and beaten on the front steps, then arrested by Roman guards, imprisoned and shipped to Rome. Then Alexander appeared in Rome and testified to Caesar against Paul. Wow!

And God said, "My grace is sufficient for thee: for my strength is made perfect in weakness."

Keep in mind that the Corinthians know who Alexander is, so in this writing to them this *thorn* is just a metaphor, not a mystery. I ask you then, how is God's strength made perfect in the weakness of Paul? Paul doesn't see it but he trusts God. See, without Alexander, Paul is just another church builder, but because of this thorn, Paul is in chains. While in chains he writes, 2nd Corinthians, Galatians, Ephesians, Philippians, Colossians, 2nd Thessalonians, 2nd Timothy, Titus, Philemon, and Hebrews. If Paul is not imprisoned and taken to Rome, there is no reason for Peter to head that way, and Sylvanus would not be there for sure, so 1st and 2nd Peter would not exist. If Paul is not in prison, there is no reason for John to be writing and delivering his messages in 1st, 2nd and 3rd John, so they would not exist. James and Jude would probably not exist. And if Paul is not in prison, there is no reason for John to go to Asia, so Revelation would not exist. If Paul were not in prison in Rome, Luke would have no reason to write the book of Acts, and since the book of Luke was possibly finished at the same time, most likely in Rome, it would not exist either. Without Alexander being a thorn in the flesh of Paul, the New Testament only has five or six books. The strength of Jesus Christ is made perfect through the weakness of Paul. Did the Word of God just wake up a little?

If you're a Bible reader how is it that you didn't see that? Is somebody's doctrine getting in the way? The way the Bible is presented, word by word, verse by verse, chapter by chapter makes this impossible to see. When read story by story, and letter by letter, just like you read any other book, the Bible will come alive. Alexander the coppersmith was a pain in the back side.

If you can see that Gnostics don't exist in the Bible, and you can see that the Epistles of John were written in the fifties by the evidence in 3rd John, and you can see the truth of the metaphors in 2nd John by the patterns in his writing, then you're ready for the fourth discernment.

5

STORY LINE

As Jesus and His followers were leaving Jericho, the blind beggar Bartimaeus, who was sitting on the side of the road, began to cry out, "Jesus, Son of David, have mercy on me." Many told him to be quiet, but he just got louder. Jesus heard him and opened his eyes.

The goal of this discernment is to help you see the things that scholars don't see. I'm going to teach you how to read again, and really, it's that simple. When you read a mystery, like Sherlock Holmes, are you constantly looking for clues? Isn't that what you do when you read a mystery? When reading an instruction manual are you focused on keeping the instructions in order? When you read a map, do you calibrate points of interest and note their location in relation to other points? When you read a translation from a foreign language, do you notice the difference in structure from your native language? You need to do all these things and more when you read the Bible. And when you read a true story, do you ponder its importance, its flair, and its character? In today's world, the Bible is nothing more than chapters and verses, and words on a page. A preacher takes two or three random verses and then finds some stories, just like in this book, and then adds church doctrine, and within thirty to sixty minutes attempts to make an alter call. The story of Jesus becomes nothing more than that, the church doctrine. And that doctrine released the Pharisees, Sadducees, and Scribes from their crimes, and in so nullified their works against the early church. Not only that, but by switching the enemy, the scholars have once again opened the door to the sway of Satan and allowed works just like those of Christ's enemy to have access. Jesus said, beware of the Pharisees, Sadducees, and Scribes, and Paul said he delivered Alexander to Satan, and John says, don't let them in your church, and the new church doctrine ignores this truth, and says in John's old age he has found the enemy of the church. It's the Gnostics. So which pew does Alexander sit in, or is he at the podium? If you know that the doctrine of the Sadducees is what John is fighting and not the doctrine of some Roman fruitcake, it makes a big difference. Sadducees don't believe in the raising of the dead. They don't believe in angels. They believe in the law of Moses. John's doctrine is the law of Jesus Christ. They are not the same. The modern church worries that a change in the doctrine of our founding fathers is somehow an attack on Jesus, but the truth is the present doctrine is an attack on Jesus. Remove the doctrine of religion, and the doctrine of Jesus is all there is. Amen? Furthermore, this Gnostic stuff, being passed as doctrine is maybe a hundred years old. That makes it modern opinion and not doctrine at all. But that opinion to modern religion is the doctrine of the church. The doctrine of Jesus is in the Gospels, and it's summarized and made completely sure in 1st John, and it's really simple.

Remember my made-up murder story where the actual murderer was set free because of the alibi given by the district attorney to the prosecuting attorney, thus sending the police to find more evidence, and in the end sentencing the second man to death because of circumstantial evidence and his lack of an alibi. When this fellow was asked about his whereabouts on the day in question, he told the authorities he was at church praying. The police asked for witnesses from the church and he said, he was praying by himself. The police took that as his cover up and assuming he was guilty, looked no further into the case. Now many years later, it has been discovered that the actual murderer is the brother-in-law of the district attorney. The district attorney's financial records show that he received a wedding gift from this guy for two hundred thousand dollars just one year before the murder, and another two hundred thousand after the murder to buy a new house. Plus, the murderer has mob ties. With this news on the street, several reporters started looking into the case and found that on the church registry, where the other fellow was praying, shows that he was indeed there at that church that day. With a little further investigating, it was discovered that this guy had a habit of buying a newspaper on the corner stand by that church upon leaving prayer time. The owner of the one man stand remembers the story of the murderer and remembers his customer very well. He just never linked the two together, and he just thought the fellow had moved on. He's telling his story to anyone that will listen. The courts are turning a sympathetic ear, but say that justice has run its course, and precedent is set, and though the decision may be wrong, there is nothing that can be done.

This made-up murder story is nothing more than a metaphorical story that shows the weakness in the doctrine of modern religion. There is no intention to change the parts of doctrine that are wrong, and what the made-up story shows us is the enemy is still influencing the church. The church has switched to this doctrine of fighting Gnostics, which allows the influence of the Pharisees, Sadducees, and the Scribes to infiltrate the church untouched, and allows them to bring their doctrine. John said, don't allow them in your church. John said don't associate with them, and religion embraces them. They nailed Jesus on a cross for asserting He was the Son of God and refusing to follow their laws. John calls them deceivers and the antichrist, and Jesus said over and over to be aware of them. Church doctrine says beware of fairytales. In 2nd John it says, "Look to yourselves, that we lose not those things which we have wrought, but that we receive a full reward." KJV. In 1st John it says, "But the anointing which ye have received from him abideth in you, and ye need not that any man teach you: but as the same anointing teacheth you of all things, and is truth, and is no lie, and even as it hath taught you, you will abide in him. And now, little children, abide in him; that when he shall appear, we may have confidence, and not be ashamed before him at his coming." KJV. John wrote these verses to combat these Sadducees that were infiltrating the church. Did I just not write, take a few scriptures, then add some stories and then work towards an alter call. If you are in fellowship with Jesus Christ then you are saved and have the anointing of the Holy Spirit. The truth I am writing in this little book, you have never heard before, but if you are in fellowship, you know that what you are hearing rings true. In 1st Thessalonians Paul writes, "Prove all things; hold fast what is good." KJV. I beg and pray that you test these things.

When I go in next month to get my two-year Department of Transportation physical that is required for all commercial drivers, I'm going to be required to take two eye exams. The first one is to check how far I can see clearly, and the second is to see if I am colorblind. If I fail either of them my job is in Jeopardy, as I would have restrictions put on my license and would lose my interstate driving privileges, costing me my job. But no worries, as I see well.

I'm going to try to describe the color-blind book that the doctor will use to test me. There will be about ten pages, and on each page of this book, is a circle about the size of a small dinner plate. In this circle there are hundreds of small circles of different sizes to completely fill the larger circle. All these smaller circles are one shade of color with a bit of variance in shade from little circle to little circle. In my example, those little circles are a shade of green. In the middle of the big circle there is a number drawn using the little circles, and in this example, we'll say it is the number 8. It's clear as day, because it is colored in the shade of a soft red. If you are color-blind and cannot distinguish reds from greens, you will not see this number 8. Furthermore, if you are wearing rose-colored glasses, you will never see the number 8 until you take off the glasses. Do you see where I'm going with this?

The Bible, to scholars is just words on paper. They see no message, and they see no story line. They doubt authenticity, and some consider people like me who actually believe the Bible to be a fool. I believe in Jesus Christ as my savior, and just like I can see the number 8 in the middle of the plate, I can see who my brother is in 1st John. Scholars treat the Bible like the plate of circles, making every word a circle and making every plate a book. The scholars can tell you how many words there are and how often each word is used. They can tell you what the Greek and Hebrew definition of the root word is and tell you where else a word like it was used. They can tell you if the fundamental sentences match anything from other periods of history and compare it to all other historical data. They can nullify any originality to the point, as in the Epistles of John, that they are not sure who the author is. They want you to see how smart they are, so they give you free rose-colored glasses. In this case that would be the commentary added to your study Bibles. If that's not enough, you can use their lexicon and concordance that neuter the Greek to a metaphor free language. The apostles may as well be cardboard cut outs. Jesus made the wise so that they can't see the number 8 on the plate of circles, and religion chose to follow their opinion instead of what the Bible says. After years of preaching a doctrine of fiction attached to the Word by scholars, nobody can see the number 8, because everybody has on the glasses. On this plate, number 8 is your brother in 1st John.

The message in 1st John is not hard to see. For newbies, it's easy to see. I can tell you what it is you're looking for and with a little focus, sure enough it's right there. But to the seasoned Bible reader, knowing already what every word means and having story upon story in the way of what John was writing, well, all that junk has to be peeled away to see the message. We all have it, including me. Think of Chuck Smith, who studied and preached fifty-two sermons in a row on the first book of John. There is no way he or his congregation would be able to focus and see this truth.

You're looking into a hologram and you've been told there is a bird catching a fish, but when the image comes in focus all you see is an old man sitting at a table with a lit candle in the middle. You are told to look harder, so finally you just say, yeah, I see it, or you just quit and assume you can't see it. Well, the fact is they can't see it, and they assume the abstract flame of the candle is the bird, and the man's thumbs on the table are the fish and are pleased that they were able to see the blur that must be the truth. You see the hologram clear as day, and everyone else is believing each other, and have no clue what the artist made. The message in 1st John is right there, and everybody is looking for something else. When I said I hope to teach you how to read the Bible, this is what I was referring to; the ability to see the letter of 1st John that the apostle wrote. This is my shot, my one try to teach.

This is what I must get you past. Because of the translation, you cannot see the letter structure. Because of verse and chapters, you cannot see the letter structure. Without knowing the time line, you cannot see the letter structure. Without knowing the story line, you cannot see the letter structure. With the present letter structure being presented the way it is, you cannot see the letter structure. With the story of Gnostics being preached by every preacher on this letter makes it impossible to see the letter structure. But you will see the letter structure.

Finding your Brother

Let's learn 1st John. There is a message to 1st John. It's the most important reason and only reason he wrote the letter, and it has all but disappeared. We are about to put that message at the forefront where it belongs. Here we go.

Step 1. Erase all belief of Gnostics in the Bible from your mind.

Step 2. Erase all ideas that John is an old man writing in AD 90.

Step 3. Realize the letter is written in the same period of time as that of Paul being thrown out of the temple and beat on the front steps. This time period is confirmed as we learned by the accounts of the letter of 3rd John.

Step 4. Have a grasp of the metaphors, just as we learned from 2nd John.

Step 5. This is a letter of correction and instruction. It was not written with the idea of reading a couple words and building a sermon. It was not designed for word for word, or verse to verse, or even chapter to chapter. It's a well-written letter for *correction*.

Step 6. This letter was written to John's home church of Jerusalem, and understand it is time-specific. It was written to correct the wrong doing by the Christian Jews dealing with Paul.

Step 7. Understand that the original readers understood *exactly* what John was saying.

Step 8. There are more patterns from the magic quilter tying all his writings. One is love one another, and another is love your brother, and they are not the same. And there are still more patterns in Johns writings that prove he was writing in these patterns.

Step 9. Understand that Paul was just thrown in prison and being held because of his belief that Jesus rose from the dead and is God. John is writing in metaphors, so there is not enough proof in the letter to give the Pharisees, Sadducees, and Scribes enough evidence to drag them all to prison.

Step 10. John has used the same principles that Jesus used to confound those on the wayside, meaning the Pharisees, Sadducees, and Scribes.

Step 11. Understand the myriad of Jews that were following Jesus and still zealous for the law that Luke writes about in Acts attend and would be part of that temple that Paul was dragged from and beaten.

Step 12. These Jews were involved in the beating of Paul in some way. Either participating, watching, or condoning the beating, which makes sense. Paul was the one turning their world upside down, bringing the Gentiles into the fold, teaching they need not follow the laws of the Jews, and now being accused of bringing uncircumcised Gentiles into the temple.

Step 13. Peter, James and John are right there. It's their neighborhood. This is their flock.

Step 14. Towards the end of the Gospel of John after the departure of Judas, Jesus said to the apostles, "A new commandment I give unto you, that ye love one another; as I have loved you, that ye also love one another. By this shall all men know that ye are My disciples, that ye have love one to another." Later in this conversation Jesus says to the apostles, "This is

My commandment, that ye love one another, as I have loved you." And again, to the apostles, "These things I command you, that ye love one another." Then in 1ˢᵗ John, John writes, "For this is the message that ye heard from the beginning, that we should love one another." And again, John writes, "And this is his commandment, that we should believe on the name of his Son Jesus Christ, and love one another, as he gave us commandment." And John wrote once more, "Beloved, let us love one another: for love is of God; and everyone that loveth is born of God, and knoweth God." And once more, "Beloved, if God so loved us, we ought also to love one another." KJV. This is from the quilter, Jesus spoke this to the apostles, and John is repeating it to the flock.

Step 15. Upon seeing the story line, understand that this letter is written in love, with correction and direction, and delivered to the Christian Jews of Jerusalem.

Step 16. Just like your little Johnny in the corner, whom you love, so you repeat your message of what not to do. That is just what John is writing to these Christian Jews. Let me show you the pattern. In the same conversation, in the Gospel of John, where Jesus repeats, love one another, towards the end He says, "These things I have spoken to you, that ye should not be offended. (made to stumble) They will put you out of the synagogues: yea, the time cometh, that whosoever killeth you will think that he doeth God service. And these things will they do unto you, because they have not known the father, nor me. But these things I have told you, that when the time shall come, ye may remember that I told you of them." KJV. Paul who watched over and condoned the stoning of Stephen, was one of those Pharisees that believed he was doing the service of God, who was confronted by Jesus on the road to Damascus, and repented, and now is an apostle of Christ. I repeat, an apostle of Jesus Christ, doing only His will, and has been dragged from the temple and beaten on the front step for false crimes, and is imprisoned for one belief, that Jesus is the Christ, and He rose from the grave, and is God! Peter, James and John sent Paul to the temple for a cleansing. Peter, James and John got an awakening, and this letter from John, is that awakening. It's a cleansing not to the laws of Moses, but to Christ. A cleansing to the new Covenant. John writes, "He that saith he is in the light, and hateth his brother, is in darkness even until now. He that loveth his brother abideth in the light, and there is none occasion of stumbling in him." And, "In this the children of God are manifest and the children of the devil: Whosoever doeth not righteousness is not of God, neither he that loveth not his brother." And, "We know that we have passed from death unto life, because we love the brethren. He that loveth not his brother abideth in death." And, "If a man say, I love God, and hateth his brother, he is a liar: for he that loveth not his brother whom he hath seen, how can he love God whom he hath not seen? And this commandment have we from Him, that he who loveth God must love his brother also. Whosoever believeth that Jesus is the Christ is born of God; and everyone that loveth him that begat also loveth him also that is begotten of him." KJV. And, who is that? Who is you brother in 1st John? His name is Paul! After every brother in these lines add Paul's name.

Step 17. The parts of the letter just written are a pattern of correction by John. They appear in the letter before or after John has given direction for the Jews that are following Jesus Christ, and makes it very clear that you cannot hate Paul and have fellowship with Christ. And that's what the whole letter is about.

All the evidence I used to get to Paul was from the Bible. It was from the books of the New Testament, and their connections to one another, and by the writings of John and his patterns with metaphors. I truly hope you see what I see. Once you see it, it's hard to deny that it is there. The evidence outside the Bible to argue against this is weak to none, but the scholarly opinion and mass of pastoral misinformation is thick, real thick, and the Bible-reading world sees a different story.

I'm going to paraphrase the letter to the first correction in 1st John. We have been with Jesus and have a relationship with God, and you may also have this fellowship; but you can't sin and have this fellowship. But walk with Jesus and your sins are removed. Confess your sins and they are forgiven. Jesus is our advocate with God and died for our sins. If you do not keep the commandments of Jesus, you are not in fellowship. Jesus said, keep my commandments, and now I write a new commandment, and he who says he follows Jesus, and hates his brother Paul, is in darkness until now. He who loves his brother Paul, abides in Jesus, and there is no cause for stumbling in him. John gives direction and follows with the correction. This pattern flows through the whole letter.

It reads just like a parent to little Johnny. John gives direction, and more direction and then he gives a reprimand. Then he makes more points and gives another reprimand. If you don't practice righteousness you're not in fellowship with God, and neither is he that does not love Paul. And then more points to the next reprimand.

And His commandment says we should believe on the name of Jesus Christ and love one another, as he gave Commandment. Then more points to the reprimand, Beloved, as Jesus loved us, we also ought to love one another. Then more points to the reprimand. If someone says, I love God, and hates Paul, he is a liar; For he who does not love Paul whom he has seen, how can he love God who he has not. And this commandment we have from Jesus, that whoever loves God must love Paul also. Whoever believes that Jesus is the Christ is born of God, and everyone who loves Jesus who was Given by the Father also loves Paul who was given by Jesus. Then more to restate the points to the end of the letter. And all points equal and amplify the message of the letter just outlined. Magic quilter indeed.

When you apply scholarly opinion and move the letter thirty to forty years later in history and make John's metaphors neutral, the letter is read just like John intended if in the hands of Roman and Jewish persecutors. That's the letter of confusion for those on the wayside. That is the letter the modern church reads today, and to try and make sense of it, they apply the Gnostic opinion, and now read a confusing love letter from John. Also because of the opinions applied to make the letter fit a religious format, it cannot be tied to the other works of John, and there is no magic. All of John's works are separate, to different events and times and locations, and the only thing tying the Bible together is the binder. In the modern church the Gospel of John is his account of the life of Jesus that ended in AD 33. The 1st Epistle of John is a love letter to a church after AD 90. The 2nd Epistle of John is to a Lady confronting Gnostics in the nineties, and the 3rd Epistle of John is to Gaius, who housed the brethren, in the nineties. The Book of Revelation is from this time period also. Just writing that makes me sad for the misinformed Bible reading world.

Let's say it's AD 90 and John wrote this Epistle. Where was he? Who did he write it to? Add all the scholarly opinion and pick a place? It's probably not Jerusalem, the city is essentially sacked and the temple burned down. Asia? Rome? No, there's a funny little block of verse that says, "I write unto you little children, because ye have known the Father." Who knew the Father? That would be the Jews. This letter was written to a group of Jews in the nineties? Twice John writes, "I have written unto you fathers, because ye have known him that is from the beginning." These fathers knew Jesus. From the first line of this Epistle, that is Jesus. Thus, in AD 90 John is writing to a group of Jews that the older members of the group knew or seen Jesus. Really? Not in Rome or Asia! In AD 90 there is a group of Jews that John writes to and says, "They went out from us, but they were not of us: for if they had been of us, they would no doubt have continued with us: but they went out, that they might be made manifest that they were not all of us." So, we can assume those that went out were Jews, and they are denying that Jesus is the Christ. John writes, "Let that therefore abide in you, which ye have heard from the beginning." That says which you heard from Jesus, and He's been off the cross for fifty-seven years in AD 90. John writes again, "For this is the message that ye heard from the beginning, that we should love one another." KJV. Hmm, anyone under seventy-five years of age would have no idea what he means. They were babies or unborn. Go to the front of John's Epistle and he writes, we heard, we seen, we handled, then just a little down he says, we declare to you. In the nineties all the other apostles were gone. John writes, that you may have fellowship with us? And these things we write to you that your joy may be full? This is the message that we heard from Him and we declare to you? Well, not in AD 90. There is no we because everybody else is dead. And scholars study everything but the Word of God! The Word of God says this Epistle was written in the fifties.

This letter, through translation and time, has become quite neutered. And then being written and read in monotone, the true message is almost lost. When you add ignorant scholarly opinion the message intended by John to the saints disappears; but it is right there, and I hope you see it, otherwise I'm a terrible teacher.

Just like those looking at my pretend hologram and see the light of the candle and say, oh a bird, and then call the thumbs of the man sitting at the table a fish, you cannot see the meaning of John's letter if you are busy trying to see the new message of Gnosticism, and as lovely and real as they tell you that it is, it's not there, it's not real, it's fiction. Just like looking at the circle of circles, if you are color-blind or wearing rose-colored glasses, you can't see the number 8 in the middle of the circle. Until you take off your preconceived ideologies of 1st John you can't see Paul. You can study every single word and every single phrase, and you won't have a clue what John said.

Just like your little Johnny smacking little Suzie in the nose makes you ponder your attitude toward your child, without the realization that 1st John is not a love letter, but a reprimand, you will not be able to see through the modern-day monotone. And just like in the made-up murder story, that is metaphorically parallel to why you cannot see Paul, if it were not for the internet and the Nag Hammadi and other modern finds like the base of the statue of Simon the accountant, the Pharisees, Sadducees, and the Scribes may have actually won the day.

I eat, drink, and sleep New King James Version, so at this point in this little book, I initially wrote 1st John in NKJV, but for copywrite reasons I changed it. As with other verses in this book, I started the transition to the King James version and realized that version just didn't communicate the same thing because of its age and style. I then decided to modernize the KJV by asserting modern English and phrasing in some places and realized about thirty percent of the time I had just rewritten the NKJV. This would obviously happen occasionally, but thirty percent of the time shows my attraction to the NKJV text, thus making it still a plagiarism. So in my attempts to be original, and still true to the Greek, I started feeling as though I were creating a Frankenstein. My goal is to make the letter of 1st John understandable. Mind you, I found Paul by reading the NKJV, and the message I'm presenting is right there, and you can find everything I'm writing in that Bible. In this version of the letter I have written, I have put emphasis on simplifying the meaning of the letter that John wrote.

There are words that are important to understanding the text of the letter. For instance, the word *abide* is a facet of John's letter that ties it all together. For a section in the King James version that same word becomes *dwelleth*. It means essentially the same thing four hundred years ago, but when you read a different word, you will assume John is referring to a different or new thing, and he's not. It's the same thing through the whole message, so it is important to continue with *abide*. Jesus told his disciples that as I abide in the Father, you will abide in me. This abide is part of the fellowship message in the letter, but if I write, Jesus said as I have fellowship with the Father, you have fellowship with me, well, that is correct but incomplete, as fellowship, and dwell, and endure, and more all fall under *abide*, making abide the correct translation.

It is also important that I keep the Greek intact for the metaphors. In my version of this letter, I have accented most metaphors and descriptions of Jesus. I have also capitalized the words that define the Father and the Holy Spirit. When you can see that a word represents Jesus, then you can understand the sentence "and truly our fellowship is with the Father and His son Jesus Christ." From this line we know that *truth* is fellowship with God. I simplify it even more for understanding purposes, to mean *truth* is fellowship with Jesus. When you see the metaphor *truth* in this letter, insert "fellowship with Jesus" and see how it makes sense.

The story line for 1st John has been lost for a long time probably because of the metaphors. It has been lost even before St. Irenaeus. When translated from Greek, many guesses were made as to what the letter was about, and the same holds true for applying the verse and chapters. I have an example with this beautiful verse number twenty-five. "The hand-picked flowers on the table smell wonderful

on my peanut butter sandwich; I also would like some grape jelly."
Verse twenty-four is about a lovely decorated table, and verse twenty-
six is a discussion about lunch. The translators of the verse did
not understand that flowers do not go on peanut butter and jelly
sandwiches, and though the translation has all the right words, they
missed the story line and sentence structure. If it were in the Bible
preachers would preach, "Oh how wonderful of a God we have
that He cares so much that He provides even flowers to enjoy on
our peanut butter and jelly sandwiches." Then the whole world
like lost sheep, walk around eating flowers. Look! The hand-picked
flowers on the table smell wonderful. Period. End of sentence, end
of paragraph, then new paragraph, and new topic. On my peanut
butter sandwich I would like some grape jelly. Because of the
metaphors, the story line and sentence structure are lost in 1st John.
I'm not writing Frankenstein, I'm dissecting it. My writing is not the
perfect enchilada. Every time I read it and study, I find room for
improvement. It is not perfect, but it's the closest to what John wrote
that's been written in a long, long time. Authors Paraphrase.

1st John

> That which was *from the beginning* that we heard,
> and we seen, and we looked upon, and our hands
> touched, aka, the *word of life*. That's the *life* that was
> given, that we seen and bear witness and declare to
> you, that *eternal life* that was with the Father and
> shared with us. That which we seen and heard we
> declare to you, so that you may also have fellowship
> with us, and in *truth*, our fellowship is with the
> Father and His son Jesus Christ.

> This we write so that your joy can be complete. This
> is the message that we heard from *him* and declare
> to you, that God is *light*. In *him* there is no darkness
> at all. If we say that we have fellowship with *him* and

walk in darkness we lie and are not practicing the *truth*. But if we walk in the *light* we have fellowship with each other.

The blood of Jesus Christ, His son washes away all sin. If we say we have no sin we fool ourselves and *truth* is not in us. If we confess our sin, *he* is faithful and just to forgive our sins and wash us from all unrighteousness. If we say we have not sinned, we make *him* a liar, and His *word* is not in us. My little children, I write these things so that you may not sin, and if you do sin, we have an *advocate* with the Father, Jesus Christ, the righteous, and *he himself* is the payment for our sins, and not only us, but the whole world.

This is how we know that we know *him*, we keep *his* commandments. He that says, I know *him*, and doesn't keep *his* commandments is a liar, and *truth* is not in him. But whoever keeps *his* words has the love of *God* truly perfected in him. This is how we know that we are in *him*. He that abides in *him*, should walk just as *he* walked. Brothers, I am not writing a new commandment to you. I'm writing the commandment you had *from the beginning*. That commandment is the word you heard *from the beginning*. This commandment that I'm writing is true in *him* and in you.

The darkness is passing away because the *true light* is already shining. He that says he is in the *light* but hates his brother is in darkness even now. He that loves his brother abides in the *light* and there is no reason for stumbling. But he that hates his brother is in darkness and walks in darkness and has no clue where he is going because the darkness has blinded him. I write you little children because your sins are forgiven through *his* name! I write you fathers because you knew *him, from the beginning*. I write you young men, because you have overcome the wicked one. I have written to you little children because you have known of the Father, and I have written to you fathers because you knew *him, from the beginning*, and I have written to you young men because you are strong and the *word* of God abides in you, and you have overcome the wicked one. Do not love the world or the things of the world! Whoever loves the world, does not have the love of the Father. For all that is of the world, the lust of flesh and the lust of eyes and the pride of life, is not of the Father, but of the world. The world is passing away with its lusts, but he that does the will of *God* abides forever.

Little children this is the last hour and you have heard that the antichrist is coming. Many antichrists are already here and by this we know that it is the last hour. They went out from us, but they were not of us, because if they had been they would have continued with us. They went out so that they could show they were not of us. You are anointed by the Holy One and know all things. I have not written to you because you don't know the *truth*, but because you know it, and no lie is of the *truth*. Who is a liar but he that denies that Jesus is the Christ? He is the antichrist that denies the Father and the *son* are one. He who denies the *son* does not have the Father. He who acknowledges the *son* has the Father. Thus, let that abide in you that you heard *from the beginning*. If what you heard *from the beginning* abides in you,

you will abide in the *son* and in the Father. The promise that *he* promised us is *eternal life*.

These things I have written to you concerning those that are trying to deceive you. The anointing you received from *him* abides in you. You don't need anyone to teach you. The same anointing teaches you of all things and is true and is not a lie. Just as it has taught you, you will abide in *him* so that when *he* appears we will have confidence and not be ashamed before *him* when *he* comes.

If you know that *he* is righteous then you know that everyone that practices righteousness is born of *him*. Behold what manner of love the Father has bestowed upon us that we can be called the children of *God*. Thus, the world doesn't know us because it didn't know *him*. Beloved, we are the children of *God*. It has not been revealed what we will be, but we know that when *he* is revealed, we will be like *him* as *he* is. Every man that has this hope in *him* purifies himself, just as *he* is pure. He who commits sin is practicing unrighteousness, because sin is unrighteousness. You know that *he* was given to take away our sins, and in *him* there is no sin. He that abides in *him* does not sin. Whoever sins has not seen *him* or known *him*. Little children, don't let them deceive you. He who practices righteousness is righteous, just as *he* is righteous.

He who sins is of the devil. The devil has sinned from the beginning. For this reason, the *son* of God was given, that *he* might destroy the works of the devil. Whoever is born of *God* does not sin because *his* seed remains in him. He does not sin because he is born of God. In this the children of God and the children of the devil are made clear. Whoever does not practice righteousness is not of God, and neither is he who does not love his brother. This is the message we heard *from the beginning*, that we should love one another. Not like Cain, who was of the wicked one and murdered his brother. And why did he murder him? Because his own works were evil and his brothers were righteous. Do not marvel my brethren if the world hates you. We know we've passed from death to life because we love the brethren. He that doesn't love his brother abides in death. He that hates his brother is a murderer, and you know that no murderer has *eternal life* abiding in him.

By this we know love, that *he* laid down *his* life for us. Thus, we should lay down our lives for the brethren. Whoever has this worlds stuff and sees his brother in need, but shuts his heart from him, how does the love of God abide in him? My little children, do not love in words or in tongue, but in deeds and in *truth*.

By this we know that we are in *truth*, that we assure our hearts before *him*. If our heart condemns us, God is greater than our heart, and knows all things. Beloved if our heart does not condemn us then we have confidence toward God. Also, what we ask, we receive from *him* because we keep *his* commandments and we do the things that are pleasing in *his* sight.

This is *his* commandment, that we should believe on the name of His *son* Jesus Christ, and love one another, as *he* gave us commandment. He who keeps *his* commandments abides in *him*, and *he* in him. We know that *he* abides in us by the Spirit that *he* has given us. Beloved, do not believe every spirit, but test the spirits to see whether they are of God, because many false prophets have gone out into the world.

By this you will know the Spirit of God, every man's spirit that confesses that Jesus Christ has *come in the flesh* is of God, and every man's spirit that does not confess that Jesus Christ has *come in the flesh* is not of God. That is the spirit of the antichrist that you heard is coming and is already in the world. You are of God little children, and have overcome them, because *he* that is in you is greater than he who is in the world. They are of the world. They speak as of the world and the world hears them. We are of God. He that knows God hears us and he that is not of God does not hear us. By this we know the spirit of *truth* and the spirit of error.

Beloved, let us love one another, for love is of God. Everyone who loves is born of God and knows God. He that does not love does not know God, for God is love. In this the love of God was made evident toward us, that God has sent His only begotten *son* into the world, that we might live through *him*. In this is love, not that we loved God, but that He loved us, and sent His *son* to be the payment for our sins. Beloved, if God so loved us, we should love one another.

Nobody has seen God at any time, but if we love one another, God abides in us, and *his* love is perfected in us. This is how we know that we abide in *him* and *he* in us, because *he* has given us *his* Spirit. And we have seen and testify that the Father sent the *son* to be the savior of the world. He that confesses that Jesus is the *son* of God has *God* abiding in him, and he in *God*. We have known and believed the *love* that God gave us. *God* is love. He who abides in love abides in *God*, and *God* in him. *Love* has been perfected among us in this, and we may have boldness in the day of judgement, because as *he* is, so are we in this world. There is no fear in love and perfect love casts out fear, because fear involves torment. He who fears has not been made perfect in *love*. We love *him* because *he* first loved us.

If anyone says, I love *God,* and hates his brother, he is a liar. If he does not love his brother whom he has seen, how can he love *God* whom he has not seen? The commandment we have from *him* is that whoever loves *God* must love his brother also. Whoever believes that Jesus is the Christ is born of *God,* and everyone that loves *him* who was begat also loves him that is begotten of *him.* By this we know that we love the children of *God,* when we love *God* and keep *his* commandments. His commandments are not hard.

Whoever is born of *God* overcomes the world. The victory that overcomes the world is our faith. Who is he that overcomes the world? He that believes that Jesus is the *son* of God! This is *he* that came by water and blood, Jesus Christ. Not by water only, but by water and blood, and it is the Spirit that bears witness because the Spirit is *truth.* There are three that bear witness from Heaven, the Father, the *word,* and the Holy Spirit, and these three are one. There are three that bear witness on earth, the spirit, the water, and the blood. These three agree as one. If we receive the witness of men, the witness of God is greater! This is the witness of God, that He testified, "This is my son". He that believes in the *son* of God has this witness in himself, and he that does not believe God has made *him* a liar, because he does not believe the testimony that God has given of His *son*. This is the testimony; God gave us *eternal life*, and this *life* is His son. He that has the *son* has *life*, and he that does not have the *son* does not have *life*.

These things I have written to you that believe in the name of the *son* of God so that you know that you have *eternal life* and so that you will continue to believe in the name of the *son* of God. This is the trust that we have in *him*, that whatever we ask in line with *his* plan, *he* hears. And if we know that *he* hears whatever we ask, then we trust in our request for forgiveness that we asked of *him*. If any man sees his brother sinning a sin that does not lead to death, have him ask, and *he* will give him life for those committing a sin not leading to death. There is a sin leading to death. I do not say that he should pray for that. All unrighteousness is sin, but there is sin not leading to death.

We know that whoever is born of *God* does not sin. He that is begotten of *God* keeps himself, and the wicked one doesn't touch him. We know that we are of *God*, and the whole world lies under the influence of wickedness.

We know that the son of God has come and given us
understanding, that we may know *him* that is *true*.
We are in *him* who is *true*, in His son Jesus Christ.
This is the true *God* and *eternal life*. Little children,
keep yourselves from the idol makers. Amen.

That is 1st John in letter form. It reads just like a letter. Alexander
is a Sadducee, and he and his boys are preaching twenty-five years
after the crucifixion of Jesus that He was just a mighty prophet. They
say that the Spirit of God landed on Him at baptism and left at His
death, so see, Jesus died and was not the Christ. John is saying in this
writing that Christ did not come through just His baptism from John
the Baptist, thus the water, but also by birth, thus the blood. John
writes that Jesus was born God as a man. This is what Christmas is
about just in case you were wondering. And we have the witness of
events to prove this. Then he goes on to say that the witness of the
Holy Spirit assures us of the Father, and the Son and the Holy Spirit,
and on earth our witness is the Spirit working in us, and the proof of
the baptism of Jesus, and the birth of Jesus. Mind you, the Sadducees
are not denying the miracles and wonders performed by Jesus, they
are just denying His Deity. God said, "This is my beloved Son, in
whom I am well pleased", God said, "This is my beloved Son: hear
him." KJV. John writes that God gave us His Son, and through Jesus
we have eternal life. That's what John writes.

John is writing to the young Christian Jews that pulled Paul from
the temple. He writes so that they may continue in Jesus and in the
promise of eternal life, so he is writing to these boys that if they
repent Jesus will hear them and forgive them. It is an awesome
Christian concept. Thank you Jesus. John writes, tell your brother
to repent.

For Paul

Four years ago, I referred to the apostle Paul as wishy-washy Paul and blamed him for a lot of the differences in religion today. In discussions with my wife, she would always defend him while I was bashing him for whatever it was that he wrote that was contradictory to what I was discussing. I considered him to be the weak link in the Gospel because of his opinions. My wife relishes in the fact that all accounts and reasons for my dislikes of Paul have been proven wrong. I understand him now. Who I used to call wishy washy, I now know to be consistent, never swayed, and strong and BRAVE. He had one message: Jesus Christ rose from the grave and is God. Everything else he did, was to share that message. I am a defender and promoter of the apostle Paul, because see, he taught me. So I'm not done with 1st John. I can't be because you might not see it yet. Lord open their eyes and give me the right words.

John writes the prepositional phrase "from the beginning" nine times in this Epistle. Eight of those times it is a metaphorical phrase for Jesus Christ, and one time it means, from the beginning. This is important, because without the understanding of this metaphor, "from the beginning" is going to be mistaken for something else. Fortunately, as with all of John's previous metaphors, he defines "from the beginning" in the very first line of the Epistle.

Early in the book, I shared that I once preached using the first of the Gospel of John, and made it say something totally different because of my inexperience to the scripture. I preached, "In the beginning was the Word, and the Word was with God, and the Word was God," KJV, to mean the Bible was the Word of God, which is way wrong. The Word, is Jesus Christ. Watch what John does with this metaphor "from the beginning." The Pharisees, Sadducees, and Scribes, want to persecute and drag Christians to Caesar, for putting Jesus as God and above Caesar. This is the crime of Paul. Watch what this quilter does. The first line of this Epistle says, "That which was *from the beginning,* that we heard and touched and seen, of the *word of life."* (paraphrased) Anybody that does not know that the "Word of life" is Jesus, does not know that "from the beginning" is Jesus, and that makes "from the beginning" in this letter mean the Law of Moses. The Pharisees, Sadducees, and Scribes would think that John is writing about the Father from the Books of Moses, but those who know the work of John know who "from the beginning" is referring to. To finish this act of confusion in the letter, John doesn't write God the Father or Jesus, but rather he uses He, Him and His. These pronouns become metaphors. I know that's not correct language, but it makes the important point. On the first page John writes, "Brethren I write no new commandment unto you, but an old commandment which ye had from the beginning. The old commandment is the word which ye have heard from the beginning. Again, a new commandment I write unto you, which thing is true in him and in you: because the darkness is past, and the true light now shineth." KJV. A Christian Jew in Johns time reads, I'm not writing a new commandment, but the old commandment you have from Jesus. This new commandment to you is true in Jesus and you, because darkness is passing away and the true light of Jesus is already shining. And that Christian understands from the letter that the command John is writing about is love one another. A Pharisee reads, brethren, I write no new commandment, but an old commandment which you heard from the beginning. He thinks what is this commandment? The commandment is the word which you heard from the beginning. The Pharisee's mind set is in the temple, hearing the words of Moses. There is no other word that gives commandment to a Pharisee, a Sadducee, or a Scribe, or any other Jew. A commandment from the beginning that was the word heard from the beginning is the law of Moses, thus this new commandment is true in him and you? Who is him? Then John says, if you hate your brother, you are in darkness, and if you love your brother you are in the light. A Pharisee thinks, what new command? Moses never said love your brother. This is crazy talk. A Christian

Jew knows that the "Word of life" is Jesus Christ, so a commandment "from the beginning" is from Jesus.

And later John writes, "And this is his commandment, that we should believe on the name of his Son Jesus Christ, and love one another, as he gave us commandment." KJV. A Christian in Johns, time knows this command, and it reads to him, "And this is Jesus commandment: That we should believe on the name of God's Son, Jesus Christ and love one another, as Jesus gave commandment." A Pharisee would read, "And this is Moses commandment from God: That we should believe in the name of God's Son Jesus Christ, and love one another, as Moses gave commandment." A Pharisee would be confused.

Then later in the letter John writes, "And this commandment have we from him, that he who loveth God love his brother also. Whosoever believeth that Jesus is the Christ is born of God: and everyone that loveth him that begat loveth him also that is begotten of him." KJV. To the Pharisee this says, and this is the commandment of God, that he who loves God must love his brother also. The Pharisee has never heard this and knows it's wrong, and to the rest has no idea. To a Jewish Christian of this time, this says, and this is the Commandment we have from Jesus, that he who loves Jesus must love his brother also. And this Christian would know that this is the old commandment that is the new commandment because Jesus never said love your brother! Open your eyes. Jesus said to the apostles, love one another. Paul is an apostle that was just pulled from the temple and beaten and arrested for believing Jesus is God. And the Christian Jews receiving this letter would know that your brother is Paul. Brother is a metaphor for the apostle Paul. And I repeat with paraphrase, "Whosoever believeth that Jesus is the Christ is born of Jesus: and everyone that loveth Jesus that was begat, loveth Paul also that is begotten of Jesus." The middle him in that sentence is your brother, and that brother is a person, and that person has a name, and his name is Paul. And the Christian Jews would know that whoever believes that Jesus is the Christ is born of God, and everyone who loves Jesus who was begotten of the Father also loves Paul who is begotten of Jesus.

Remove all metaphors and this line paraphrased says, "And this is the commandment we have from Jesus, that he that loves Jesus must love Paul also. Whoever believes that Jesus is the Christ is born of Jesus, and everyone who loves Jesus who was begotten also loves Paul who is begotten of Jesus." If you make the Him metaphors say something else it becomes jibberish! We have made it say something else but open your eyes and see the letter. Test all things. Focus in and test this if you do not believe. Test the word of God right here.

This part of the reprimand by John starts here with, "If a man say, I love God, and hateth his brother, he is a liar." KJV. This section of scripture right here is about your brother. These lines written by John are about your brother. It says how can you love Jesus who you can't see if you don't love your brother who you see. So, if it's not Paul, define brother! Well, do you think fellow Christian? The next line says, the commandment from Jesus is whoever loves Jesus must love his brother also. In this case, you say love one another also, so why didn't John just write that, like he did one page earlier. Why change from love one another to love your brother? This commandment that Jesus never said, this love your brother is a new commandment. So, why did John say it if it's just the same? John said he was giving a new commandment that was the same as the old commandment, so what is the purpose of the new commandment if it is exactly the same? Why did he write the new commandment if there is no reason?! And then I'll paraphrase the next line, "Whosoever believes that Jesus is the Christ is born of Jesus; and everyone that loves him (Jesus) who was begot also loves him (Paul) who is begotten of him (Jesus)." In the NKJV that middle him isn't capitalized. Jesus can't be the little him. Paul is the little middle him.

The prior evidence that John is writing in metaphors, itself, proves that your brother in 1st John is a metaphor. I showed you the patterns of John with the metaphors and how the evidence for them is obvious because John spelled out the meaning earlier in his writings. The evidence for your brother is a little different. The pattern is built within the letter. He says he is giving a new commandment that is an old commandment from Jesus. Then he builds on a brother theme in a time when his letter recipients are aware of the situation with Paul and know exactly what he is writing about. This letter was not written as a Gospel or for edification, but to address and fix a problem in the church. Then John gives the commandment of Jesus, which is to love Him and love one another. And then he modifies the command of Jesus to say, love your brother. When you know the time of the letter and the purpose for the letter, it becomes obvious that Paul is your brother. To think this letter is written forty years later as a love letter, thus, you must love your brother makes no sense.

In the conversation in the Gospel of John, after Judas left, Jesus said to the apostles several times to love one another. And He said, you did not choose Me, but I chose you. And He said, they will put you out of the synagogues, and kill you thinking it a service to God. Then at the end of the conversation He prayed to the Father. In that prayer, Jesus said, "And the glory which thou gavest me I have given them; that they may be one, even as we are one: I in them, and thou in me, that they may be made perfect in one; and that the world may know that thou hast sent me, and hast loved them, as thou hast loved me." KJV. John didn't just write these things, he believed and practiced them. The letter of 1st John is that action in progress.

The points made and the corrections given to the Christian Jews in Jerusalem called the 1st Epistle of John.

> **Point 1**. We walked with Jesus and He is God, and
> we have fellowship with him, and you can have this
> fellowship, with the Father and the Son. 1:1-4

Point 2. Jesus is light and there is no darkness in Him, so you cannot have fellowship and walk in darkness. Walk in the light and the blood of Christ cleanses all your sins. 1:5-7

Point 3. Confess your sins and He forgives. Deny your sins and Jesus is not in you. If we sin Jesus is our advocate before God. 1:8-2:2

Point 4. Keep Jesus' commandments. If you don't the truth is not in you. Those who keep the word of Jesus have the love of Jesus perfected in him. 2:3-6

Point 5. I'm clarifying a commandment of Jesus. 2:7-8

Correction 1. He who hates Paul is in darkness till now. He who loves Paul abides in the light and there is no correction needed. 2:9-11

I write to the church because your sins are forgiven. (point 3)

I write to the elders because you knew Jesus. (point 1&5)

I write to the new believers because you have overcome the wicked one. (point4)

I write to the church because you knew the Father. (point1)

I write to the elders because you knew Jesus. (point 1&5)

I write to the new believers because the word of God abides in you, and you have overcome the wicked one. (point 4) 2:12-14

Do not love the world. If you love the world the "love of the Father", (which is Jesus given by Him) is not in you. (point 1&2) 2:15-17

Point 6. The antichrist is coming, and some have already come from Asia, led by Alexander. They pretended to be of us but they are not. 2:18-19

Point 7. You have an anointing from the Holy Spirit to show you the truth. If they deny that Jesus is the Son of God they are the antichrist. They do not have the Father. Jesus said the only way to the Father is through Him. Trust your anointing. 2:20-28

Point 8. Practice righteousness. Do not sin. If you sin, you are not of Jesus. 2:29-3:9

Correction 2. Whoever does not practice righteousness is not of God, nor is he who does not love Paul. 3:10

Example- Cain and Able. 3:11-12

Correction 3. Don't marvel if the other Jews hate you. You have passed from death to life because we love one another. If you don't love your brother Paul, you abide in death. There is no eternal life for you. (point 4&7) 3:13-15

Correction 4. Jesus died for us, and we should lay down our lives for each other. If you see your brother in need and do not help, how does the love of Jesus abide in you. You cannot love in words, but in actions and truth. (point 2&8) 3:16-17

Correction 5. If you have done wrong and know it, Jesus is greater than your sin, so ask forgiveness, and He will forgive, because we keep the commandments of Jesus. (point 3&4) 3:18-22

Point 9. Test the spirits to see if they are of God. Every spirit that confesses that Jesus came in the flesh is of God. (point 1&7) 3:24-4:6

Point 10. Love one another. God gave his only begotten son for us. (point1&5) 4:7-11

Point 11. We have fellowship with Jesus by the gift of the Holy Spirit, and we testify that God sent His Son as the Savior of the world. You confess this and you are in fellowship. There is no fear in love. (point 1&8) 4:12-19

Correction 6. If someone says I love God, and hates Paul, he is a liar, for he who does not love his brother Paul, who is an apostle of Jesus, who we have seen, how can he love God whom he has not seen. (Jesus said in the Gospel of John, that as I loved you, love one another, and by this they will know that you are my disciples, by your love for one another.) This is Johns abbreviated new commandment from Jesus, that he who loves God must love his brother Paul also. Whoever believes that Jesus is the Son of God and loves Jesus whom was given by God also loves Paul who was given by Jesus. (point 5) 4:13-5:1

Letter summary

Point 12. We know that we love one another, when we love God we keep Jesus' Commandments. They are not burdensome. 5:2-3

Point 13. Faith in Jesus Christ overcomes the world. 5:4-5

Point 14. Jesus is the Son of God. The Father, the Word, and the Holy Spirit bear witness in heaven and are one. The Spirit, the water and the blood bear witness on earth, and all three agree. Gods witness is greater than Alexanders, and this is what God says; he who believes in the Son of God has a witness in himself. God has given us eternal life through His son. If you have the Son, you have eternal life. I write this so that you may continue to believe, because some are in sin. 5:6-12

Correction 7. If you ask according to the will of Jesus, He hears you. And we know that He forgives. If you know that your brother is in sin have him pray, and ask for forgiveness, but not for sin that separates us from God. 5:13-17

Finish line. Those born of God do not sin; but walk like Jesus, and the wicked one does not touch him. We are of Jesus and the whole world is under the sway of the wicked one. We know the Son of God has come and gave us understanding so we know what is true and are in Him who is true; In His Son Jesus Christ. This is the true God and eternal life. Keep yourself from the idol makers. Amen. 5:18-21

6

RECALL

There was a blind man in the temple that Jesus healed on the Sabbath. The Pharisees interrogated the man about his sight and then after questioning his parents, called on the man again, and told him that he must give God the glory for his sight, and not this man Jesus, as we know that he is a sinner. The man answered, whether he is a sinner or not I do not know, but one thing I do know, that I was blind and now I see. The Pharisees cast him out!

Now that you can see there are no Gnostics, and the Gospel and Epistles of John are not from the nineties, and understand the metaphors and know the story line, it is easy to see your brother. At least I hope it is. The only thing really in the way now is religion. Those of us in fellowship believe that Jesus Christ is the Son of God and abide in Him. We've got that part down. Eternal life with God is not an issue. But what we believe to get there is exposed and makes truth a little tougher or possibly easier, depending on your preferred religion. This is where you find out how much of a hold the Pharisees, Sadducees, and the Scribes actually have on you.

Just so you understand where I'm at, this whole chapter did not exist when I started writing last year. We made it through the four discernments and I planned to finish in the next chapter. Then this thing kept growing. My intention was to stay on track, but apparently this one more lap around the truth of your brother is necessary. I truly hope someone is still out there reading and finding this stuff interesting. I probably lost average Joe, and apathy Joe long ago. Hey, let's be real, I'm quoting truth from the Bible, and the world can't get past the front page.

My daughter is now twenty-one, but for application purposes, I'm stepping back six years. I'm going to write a note to my fifteen-year-old daughter. She has been given the responsibility of doing the dishes on Tuesday night, and for the last two weeks has not completed the task. The heart of my note has got to make this point: "If the dishes aren't done Tuesday night, you will be grounded this weekend." It's a Sunday afternoon, and because I work evenings, and my daughter has school, I will not see her between now and then. So the easiest thing to do would be to write a note on the small to-do list on the fridge. That was the normal practice for our house, but the last couple times of communicating responsibilities in this fashion have resulted in excuses and half-done chores. Therefore, I chose to make the note more personal. It ends up looking like this.

> Dear Alice,
>
> At the last family meeting, with everyone present, chores were assigned in an appropriate and fair manner so that no great burden would be placed on any one individual. You received no more and no less than that of your siblings. Prior to this meeting, your part of the workload was substantially more, but with your brother being more responsible now and wishing the opportunity to earn an allowance, that which is expected of you is less. In the past you

set a grand example for your brother which spurred him to wanting the same benefits you receive for participating in the family workload.

At this last meeting, I did not try to lessen the value of your chores by the fact that you now have less, and at the same time I have to compensate your brother equally for the efforts he is showing. From my standpoint, the cost for the same work has doubled, and on your part for the last two weeks, the work negotiated and expected from you has not been completed.

You agreed to doing the dishes on Tuesday night. You assured us that it would not be a problem. For the last two weeks, I have got up Wednesday morning and had to clean the kitchen. When you don't do your part, that leaves the burden on myself or your brother to clean up what was your responsibility. I was told that you left the mess because you thought it was unfair that big meals were being cooked on Tuesday and that on your brother's night to clean it is often take out. This is not on purpose, it is just how the family schedule has been working lately, and honestly, that is just an excuse to be lazy. I expect more from you than that. You have no good excuse for not doing your chores. I do not want to write a letter every time you choose to not do your chores, so we are going to have to make a new rule. This rule will be enforced on all of us to make it fair. If you fail to do any part of your chores, you will not receive an allowance on payday.

Let me remind you of what is expected. The dishes need to be washed and put away. The table and counters need to be cleaned off, and the floor needs to be swept. Don't worry about the garbage, as that is my job, so leave it.

I have written this letter because I want you to know that I am serious about this issue. To make my point, I am putting my foot down right here. If the dishes are not done on Tuesday, you will be grounded this weekend. I will be home all weekend, and maybe we need to have some family time. So if you're just dying to spend more time with me, it's going to happen if you don't do your chores. I love you and will see you on Friday.

There are a few things I want to compare from this note that turned into a short letter to my daughter, and 1st John. The first is my use of the word *brother*. There is no doubt in this note that my daughter knows exactly who her brother is, even though I never mention his name. In the letter of 1st John there is no doubt that the readers know that their brother in the letter is Paul. The second comparison is that I made several points in the letter to Alice, and all of them point directly to the purpose of the letter, being, "If you don't get the dishes done on Tuesday you will be grounded this weekend." This same concept applies for the letter of 1st John. John makes several points and they all point directly to the purpose of the letter, which is, "If you don't love your brother Paul, you're not in fellowship with Jesus." The third comparison is the same as just written, the letter to Alice could be summed up in one line: "Do the dishes on Tuesday or you are grounded this weekend." John's letter summed up in one line says, "If you don't love Paul, you are not in fellowship with God." The fourth comparison is that in my letter to Alice, my daughter and son would understand that the new rule is, "If you don't finish your chores, there is no allowance and your grounded." In 1st John the Christian Jews would understand the new commandment is, "If you don't love Paul, you're not in fellowship with Jesus," and they can see that it is not a new command, but just the enforcement of what Jesus said. The fifth comparison is this. In my letter to my daughter, change the word *family* to union, *siblings* to co-workers, *chores* to work, *brother* to associate, and *allowance* to income. All of these are appropriate synonyms. Now this letter says something completely different. It would be confusing and have something to do with violations of labor laws and retraining. There would now be no absolute idea of what the letter is about because the points are contradicting. You cannot hold one's pay and also insist they put in over time. Unless you know that John wrote in metaphors, you read a completely different letter, and book translators have translated the wrong letter. Not only is that letter confusing and contradictory, but your one line says something like, "Love one another, and obey the law of Moses."

NKJV Rules

Early in this little book I explained that I use NKJV for a reason, and that I find the modern Bibles as part of the understanding problem, especially in 1st John. You cannot see what I am going to show from the other modern translations. Thus, let's get to addressing that.

There are several models of cars right now that have a faulty air bag system made by Takata. These air bags do not work properly. Nothing like the last line of defense in an auto accident not working. These air bags can explode in a minor fender bender and throw metal slivers into drivers and passengers. This has spurred the largest safety recall in history. To resolve this problem with your automobile, the auto makers have a recall on the product. As an owner of one of the vehicles, you would take it to your dealer and they would fix it at the cost of Takata. But what is my point with another story?

My NKJV Bible that I've used to learn who your brother is, is one of the few Bibles left that you can actually see the truth of the Epistles of John with. Once the truth is revealed, it can be seen in any version, but you cannot find this truth in any version, and I find that real scary. The 1979 NKJV is a translation from the same source as the KJV with modern language. The emphasis was to be a word for word translation with the Greek that it was translated from. They used a style called complete equivalence. To translate word for word and make a modern sentence from ancient Greek is quite a challenge, but in doing this, the metaphors and metaphorical phrases used by John have stayed intact. They are all still there. This is absolutely not the case with your modern Bible.

The NKJV is translated from the Textus Receptus, which is the translation printed by Erasmus in 1516 and edited and perfected by the scholars of that day to what they believed to be the best translation of the New Testament. Wherever this translation differs from the translation of the other major Greek texts, a note is made in the margins, and you can easily compare the differences, thus totally reassuring yourself to the meaning and possible differences. These are very minimal and practically meaningless to the average Bible student, so how could it make so much difference?

In 1881, scholars were given a complete copy of the New Testament that is older than all the partial copies and fragments used by Erasmus and early scholars, and thus deemed it the most accurate. Mind you, it is also one of the manuscripts that the NKJV compares to in the columns, so overall, by all standards, it's the same book. Isn't that great news. This copy of the New Testament is the copy all modern Bibles are based upon. Then what's the problem? The modern Bible scholars don't translate word for word from the Greek. They use a new thing called dynamic translation. Instead of focusing on the Greek words, they focus on the authors intent and insure that the phrases of each passage align with the next passage. Furthermore, if they see something they believe to be repetitious they remove it. I'm not making this up. And since they're so smart, when they are done, they compare it to nothing because they have now created what is sold as the very best translation of the Bible. You can't see what 1st John says because the scholars changed it for you.

In 1881, the *Codex Vaticanus* became available as transcript as the oldest complete New Testament text. Scholars took that text and compared it to several other late texts and made adjustments to create the most accurate text. Then scholars took their best ever created Greek text and rechecked it using modern translation tools and made it even a better text by removing repetitions and other possible errors by past scribes. To ensure that you have the best copy of the New Testament ever, they translate it for you using their modern methods, and fix all the hard to understand parts to make the very best translation ever. Chances are that if you are a Bible reader, you have one of these well-marketed best translation ever Bibles. And like I said, now you can't see your brother Paul in 1st John. Keep in mind how I changed a handful of words in the letter to my daughter and it easily became a new thing. We are about to have that happen in the modern Bible versions in 1st John. Are you thinking, oh, how could this make a big difference? If John writes in a pattern of metaphors and you change the word to another word, or remove the word, it makes a big difference!

I'm going to discuss the scripture I shared in chapter one. In 1st John 5:1 it says, "Whosoever believeth that Jesus is the Christ is born of God: and everyone that loveth him that begat loveth him also that is begotten of him." KJV. The appropriate Greek word for the middle *him* is him. Modern translation changed the word to child, children, his child, and whoever is born of him, all being references to Jesus. Those are all different from *him*, especially when *him* is a metaphor for Paul. I will show why this happens with another example using 1st John 2:7. In the KJV (italics added) it says, "Brethren, I write no new commandment unto you, but an old commandment which ye had *from the beginning*. The old commandment is the word which ye have heard *from the beginning*." In this verse the metaphorical phrase, *from the beginning* is used twice, and both times is a reference to Jesus. It says, Brethren, I'm giving you a commandment that you received from Jesus and heard from Jesus. And that commandment is "love one another." I say this now because in the next bit it will get lost in the alternate message.

Now this verse has them asterisks in the NKJV, meaning a change from the NU-text in two places. NU-text is the text published in the twenty-seventh edition of the Nestle-Aland Greek New Testament, and in the United Bible Societies' fourth edition, and from those we get the acronym, "NU-text." That essentially means the text used for the modern Bibles in 1979. The first change is from *Brethren* to Beloved, and the second is to remove the second *from the beginning*. The NIV, NLT And NASB all change *Brethren* to something else, and the NLT and NIV change the phrase *from the beginning* that represents Jesus to something else, and they all remove the second *from the beginning*. So now the metaphor in John's letter that represents Jesus has been removed and the letter says something new, and that is follow the laws of Moses. The sentence before in the KJV says, "He that saith he abideth in him ought himself also so to walk, even as he walked." Yet, to assist the interpretation of the modern Bible, in this sentence the NLT changed the word *him* to God and the NLT and the NIV both changed the third *he* to Jesus. Now this sentence in context to the next sentence using dynamic translation, makes it say to live with the Father you have to walk like Jesus, and in the next two sentences you have to follow the commandments from Moses. Those lines in the KJV and the NKJV say that to abide in Jesus you should walk like Jesus. And then it says, I'm not writing a new commandment, it is the same one you got from Jesus. The commandment is what you heard from Jesus. If you put the *him* and *he* in the NLT and NIV translations where the scholars have substituted an alternate word, it will say, that he who abides in Jesus walks like Jesus.

When you change a couple words, and remove a couple words and rearrange the phrasing, the letter is going to say something different.

The intention of the scholars with this interpretation is to say to follow the Commandments of the Father, which are the laws of Moses that have been complicated by the Pharisees, Sadducees and the Scribes. These are the laws that Jesus ignored and was crucified for. John wrote that they sought to kill him for healing on the Sabbath and claiming to be the Son of God. Yet, the very next line in the NIV after it says follow the commandments of the Father, tells us that we are to live for the truth of the commandments just like Jesus did. That assures the commandments are from Father God in the Bible. But Jesus broke those laws? He died on the cross to fulfill that old covenant? Just a small handful of words were translated differently to make the phrasing of the letter read more clearly and the whole thing has changed.

My Bible says that if you follow Jesus you should walk like Jesus, and I'm giving you a command that you received and heard from Jesus. Those Bibles say, to live with the Father you must live as Jesus did. And the command is from the Father. Those are two different things. One says follow Jesus and obey His commandments, and the other says, live with the Father and obey His commands. How do you know which one is right? It's easy you know. The Gospel of John is the instruction manual. It has all the answers to all the questions in 1st John. John wrote both books and used the same words, so it is easy to understand one book by the answers from the other. Everything John wrote says the same thing. Every answer for 1st John can be found in the Gospel of John, in chapter one and chapters thirteen through nineteen. Essentially in the opening of the Gospel, and right after Judas left is where you find the instructions to fill in all the *Hims* and other metaphors and understand what John means. These are not sort of, kind of, ring around the rosy, maybe answers. These are direct obvious answers, but remember, this only works with the NKJV or older Bibles, because the modern versions changed the Greek words using the dynamic translation method.

Let's look at 1st John 5:1 again. When you know the time line of the letter written, and the reason for the letter, and the purpose and correct answers for the metaphors in the letter, you know that this sentence says in the KJV: "Whosoever believeth that Jesus is the Christ is born of God: and every one that loveth him (Jesus) that (*was*) begat loveth him (Paul) also that is begotten of him (Jesus)." That is what a Christian Jew from Jerusalem read in AD 57. When you know the middle *him* in this sentence is Paul, you have a grasp of the whole letter, and you have the knowledge to combat the Pharisees, Sadducees, and the Scribes. Let me show you again why it matters. When you know that the middle *him* is Paul, then the *him* prior and after the middle *him* must be Jesus. Then the next sentence says, this is how we know the followers of Jesus, by keeping the commandments of Jesus. That commandment once again being referenced is "love one another". This is John's point. Jesus told the apostles, to love one another, and John is writing if you don't love Paul, who is an apostle, you're not in fellowship with Jesus because this is Jesus' commandment. When you see Paul, everything else is easy to understand and see. If you remove Paul and replace the middle *him* with Jesus or a metaphor, synonym, or other name for Jesus, and make the outside *hims* mean Father God, well, now you're telling a different story.

The modern versions say, his child, children and child for the middle *him*. The Textus Receptus and the other translations are the exact same in the Greek on this verse. These are all translation modifications to make a better Bible, and this is what you get. When the middle *him* becomes Jesus, in the next sentence the children of God becomes Jesus, and the commandments become the law of Moses. To be in fellowship with Jesus in these modern Bibles, you have to adhere to the laws of the Pharisees, Sadducees, and the Scribes. Because you don't know the metaphors, this law can be confirmed in the modern Bible three more times in 1st John. I already showed you two of them, and for the other two you just need to go to where it says, *from the beginning*. The first of the book says, paraphrased, "That which is from the beginning that we heard and seen and looked at and touched is the Word of life." Well, if it's not Jesus, the Word of life must be the law of Moses. In the modern Bible right after Jesus becomes the child, it says obey Gods commandments, and then it says Gods commandments are not burdensome, and that is confusion maximus in the Word of God. Jesus died on the cross to fulfill the old covenant. He died for my sins, and by the modern Bible translation I have to earn my salvation through works. What did Jesus die for? So, the gift of Christ is just a door greeting? By this translation the old covenant is still in effect. The modern Bible has allowed the Pharisees, Sadducees, and Scribes to manage your salvation, while you search the scriptures to fight the Gnostics. There needs to be a Bible recall. If the world can recall your car and fix a faulty part just to make it safer, why would you allow someone to read a book that is promising eternal life, then have a section at the end that steals that prize? Which life is more important, worldly or heavenly? I understand half the Christian world believes that John is saying follow the commandments of the Father. My only agenda is truth, and I answer only to God, and 1st John is saying two different things.

So how do I know what to believe? It's not hard. I look for answers in the Bible. John wrote this letter, and John wrote the Gospel of John, which is the ultimate instruction manual for this letter. The answer to every single real metaphor that describes Jesus is on the first page of John. These metaphors were used in duplicate in 1st John. The magic quilter writes, *from the beginning* eight times to describe Jesus and three times in pairs, and this is confirmed by John 1:1-2, which says, "In the beginning was the Word", and then "The same was in the beginning with God," then 1st John 1:1 says, "That which was from the beginning." When John writes *from the beginning* he is describing Jesus. The word *life* is repeated in 1st John 1:2 and is obviously the same *life* referred to in John 1:4 that says, "In Him was life and the life was the light of men." That life is Jesus. The word *truth* is used in 1st John 1:6,1:8, and several more times, and to confirm this as Jesus, John 1:9 says, "That was the true light which lighteth every man that cometh into the world." In John 1:14 it ends, "Of the only begotten of the Father, full of grace and truth." In the instruction manual Jesus said, "I am the way, the truth, and the life: no man cometh unto the Father, but by me." And Jesus said to Pilate, "Everyone that is of the truth heareth my voice." And John writes in 1st John 1:3, "Truly our fellowship is with the Father, and with his Son Jesus Christ." Pilate said, "What is truth?" *Truth* is fellowship with Jesus; *truth* is Jesus. The word *light* is used in 1st John 1:5,7 and 2:8,9,10 and John 1:4,9 and confirm that Jesus is the *light*. The phrase *come in* the *flesh* is used in 1st John 4:2,3 and is confirmed as a metaphor in John 1:14. It says, "And the Word was made flesh, and dwelt among us, and we beheld his glory, the glory as of the only begotten of the Father, full of grace and truth." *Come in the flesh* is God born amongst us, which is Jesus. John writes, "Every spirit that confesseth that Jesus Christ is come in the flesh is of God:" KJV. A Sadducee can't touch this with a ten-foot pole as evidence against Christians because a Sadducee also worships God, so Caesar could persecute him also. But if John writes, every spirit that confesses that Jesus Christ is God and walked among us, well, that's just what Paul is being held by the Romans for, and this letter is written to condemn the Christian Jews for having a part in. Furthermore, the enemy that had Paul thrown from the temple is still lurking, thus John writes in metaphors. It's not a secret code, it's protection for the believer. Let's say you're a follower of Jesus in this time, and you have been armed with this wisdom from John, and a centurion with a group of Sadducees comes up and corners you and tests your loyalty to Caesar. They ask who do you worship? You say, I obey the laws of Caesar. The centurion says, these Sadducees say you place your God above Caesar. You reply, I place my God no higher than the God of the Sadducees. The centurion asks, then who is Jesus? You reply, Jesus came in the flesh, and is the Son of God, the same God as the Sadducees. John has neutralized the threat of the enemy, and it's not the Roman.

The confirmation of every single point made in 1st John can be found in the conversation Jesus had with the eleven apostles immediately after Judas left, and up to the point of Him being a prisoner of Pilate, where Pilate says, "What is truth?" Everything else in the Gospel of John furthermore confirms the points of 1st John. The whole book of John confirms who the enemy is. In John, he writes two stories where Jesus healed somebody in the Synagogue on the Sabbath, and this was a violation of the law of the Pharisees, Sadducees, and Scribes. First when Jesus was in Jerusalem, there was a man with an infirmity for thirty-eight years, and Jesus asked him if he wanted to be made well? And that day was the Sabbath. Then Jesus said, "Rise, take up thy bed, and walk." Then a few sentences later John wrote, "And therefore did the Jews persecute Jesus, and sought to slay him, because he had done these things on the sabbath day. But Jesus answered them, My Father worketh hitherto, and I work. Therefore the Jews sought the more to kill him, because he not only had broken the sabbath, but said also that God was his Father, making himself equal with God." KJV.

Then again while stirring the pot with the Pharisee, Sadducee, and Scribes, He said to them, "Verily, verily, I say unto you, Before Abraham was, I am." John then writes, "Then they took up stones to cast at him: but Jesus hid himself, and went out of the temple, going through the midst of them, and so passed by." The next line says, "And as Jesus passed by, he saw a man who was blind from his birth." He healed this man also and it was on the Sabbath. Then the next time He came to the temple the Jews surrounded Him and said to Him, "If thou be the Christ, tell us plainly." Jesus started with, "I told you, and ye believed not:" And He finished with, "I and my Father are one." This sent the Jews to picking up stones again. And again, Jesus escaped from their grasp. The next thing He did was raise Lazarus from the dead. This caused the Pharisees and the Chief Priests to gather, and John writes, "Then from that day forth they took counsel together for to put him to death." KJV.

The enemy of Jesus, from the pen of John, are the Pharisees, Sadducees, and the Scribes. The crimes of Jesus are claiming to be the Son of God and working miracles on the Sabbath. Why would John write these things of all the things he could have written about Jesus, that absolutely show that the Son of God not only had contempt for what the Pharisees, Sadducees, and Scribes had done to the law, but went out of His way to break their laws to the point of them wanting to kill Him. Why would John write that and then write a letter that says follow the law of Moses? He would not do that!

We are not talking about the Ten Commandments here. The commandments of Jesus encompass the Ten Commandments. We are talking about the laws of the Pharisees, Sadducees, and Scribes and the old covenant. Jesus' commandments were simple and not burdensome. Love your God, love your neighbor, and all the others fall under these. And then Jesus told His apostles to love one another. Those are the commandments of Jesus. If you make 1st John say the commandments of the Father, then you reestablish the old covenant, which are the Laws of Moses that are indeed burdensome. To be a child of God you must be circumcised. You must tithe. There are pages of things you cannot eat. There are many feasts you must partake in. You can do no work on the Sabbath. For all your sins and transgressions, you must bring them to your local Pharisee and he will for a fee, take them before the Lord. Without these laws and much more, you are not in fellowship.

Jesus died to fulfill that covenant! Jesus is the new covenant. So what does the instruction manual say? Right after Judas leaves in the conversation with the eleven, Jesus says, "A new commandment I give unto you, That ye love one another; as I have loved you, that ye also love one another." And He said, "If ye love me, keep my commandments." And He said, "He that hath my commandments, and keepeth them, he it is that loveth me: and he that loveth me shall be loved of my Father, and I will love him, and will manifest myself to him." And He said, "If a man love me, he will keep my words; and my

Father will love him, and we will come unto him, and make our abode with him." And He said, "If ye keep my commandments, ye shall abide in my love; even as I have kept my Father's commandments, and abide in His love." And He said, "This is my commandment, That ye love one another, as I have loved you." And He said, "These things I command you, that ye love one another." KJV. All that is within three pages of the instruction manual. By the manual, we know that we are to keep the commandments of Jesus.

If you read the first page of John to 1:14 and the instruction manual, John 13:31-18:38, and understand the metaphors, and know the time frame, then this letter makes total sense. I have shown you other patterns from the magic quilter and how he knits, and this here is a formula for even more patterns. For instance, when he writes abide, or manifest, to really understand the meaning, you go to the instruction manual, and just like Jesus' commandments, you will know exactly what John is writing about. I want to show a couple more patterns.

At 1st John 2:12-14 the quilter writes a repetitive section to little children, fathers and young men. The two lines to the fathers are the same. Both of these lines have the metaphorical phrase, *from the beginning*. That line reads, "I write unto you, fathers, because ye have known him, *that is* from the beginning." John used the same line defining Jesus as *from the beginning* twice on purpose. John duplicates this metaphorical phrase in back-to-back sentences two more times in this letter. By knowing that he is intentionally writing this phrase two more times in a sentence where one could easily be sufficient, he is reassuring the Christian Jews reading it, that *from the beginning* means Jesus Christ, thus making it a key to understanding the letter. I've already showed what happens if you miss this key and don't have the instruction manual. John wrote in duplicate on purpose. It is a key to the metaphors for Jesus.

This same scripture, 1st John 2:12-14, after each writing acknowledgement, says "because". It starts, "I write unto you, little children, because…" In the NKJV, *because* is capitalized all six times. Do you know why? It's part of the reprimand. Right before this part, John writes that if you don't love Paul, you're in darkness. Right after this part, John writes, do not love the world. In the church world we split these into three sections with three different topics, all about three different things, but John never stopped on the one thing. There is one point and one reprimand. This 2:12-14, is not a love greeting. Just like the reprimand to little Johnny, John is repeating himself to get their attention. The NKJV capitalized the *because*, because John's writing emphasized it, but the translators didn't understand why. Instead of the capitalization to emphasize *because*, just throw three exclamation points on the end of each line. This is a reprimand!!! So what does it say? Here is the correct dynamic paraphrased translation.

> "But he who hates Paul is not in fellowship with Jesus, and is in the sway of the wicked one, and does not know where he is going, because the Jews from Asia, with Alexander have turned you from that fellowship.
>
> I'm writing to you church, *because* your sins are forgiven by Jesus!!! I'm writing to you elders, *because* you knew Jesus Christ!!! I'm writing to you young Christians, *because* you have overcome the world!!! I'm writing to you church, *because* you know Jesus is of the Father!!! I'm writing to you elders, *because* you knew Jesus Christ!!! I'm writing to you young Christians, *because* you are strong, and you have fellowship with Jesus, and have overcome the world!!! So, do not love the world or the things of the world!!!"

I added the pertinent information, so you could see the true sentiment of the writing.

Just as the Christian Jews knew that your brother in 1ˢᵗ John was Paul and why John was writing in metaphors, and had no problem understanding each reference to Jesus, they also had no doubt who the enemy was that John was writing about. I have stated his name several times already, but I will put some proof to the letter so you can understand like the Christian Jews of John's time. Alexander is the leader of the Jews from Asia that showed up and had Paul removed from the temple and beaten at the front step. In 1ˢᵗ Corinthians when Paul says, "If after the manner of men I have fought with beasts at Ephesus," he is referring to Alexander the coppersmith. Paul writes Timothy and says that some have rejected the faith and suffered shipwreck, and I delivered them to Satan, of whom were Alexander and Hymenaeus. And it was Alexander that came forward to assist the Dianna worshippers in the coliseum in Ephesus during the riot against Christians. When John writes, "Even now are there many antichrists," he is writing about Alexander. John uses the word *they* twice in 1ˢᵗ John to refer to Alexander and his gang. "They went out from us, but they were not of us:" is a reference to the Jews of Asia. And again, John writes, "Because greater is he that is in you, than *he* that is in the world." (accent added). That accented *he* is Alexander. The next sentence says, "They are of the world." To confirm that John is talking about Alexander, the last statement in his letter is, "Little children, keep yourselves from idols." Alexander by trade, is an Idol maker.

This is another pattern of the quilter. He writes in the first of 1ˢᵗ John, "Truly our fellowship is with the Father and with His Son Jesus Christ". Every time in this letter that John is referring to the Father with a *He* or *His*, somewhere in that block of sentences, John will write, *His Son*. Otherwise, the Father is referred to as the Father.

Jesus spoke in parables to confound the wise; those that were on the wayside. Furthermore, He gave the meaning of the metaphors to the disciples so that they would understand and be edified. All the times Jesus spoke, He never said, I am God. When He was in chains before the high priest, when asked, "Art thou then the Son of God?", Jesus answered, "Ye say that I am." For this He was crucified. Everything Jesus said or did proved He was God, and He was killed by the Pharisees, Sadducees, and Scribes for it. John writes a Gospel describing his time with Jesus, and in the first fourteen versus he never uses His name, but those sentences are full of descriptions of Jesus. Full of metaphorical descriptions that describe Jesus as God. When John writes 1st John, he uses all these metaphorical descriptions to represent Jesus. He never writes Jesus is God, because that, especially right at this time, could be used as a weapon by the Pharisees, Sadducees, and the Scribes. But if you know the metaphors, the whole letter says Jesus is God. 1st John never openly says Jesus is God, and says nothing less than Jesus is God.

I went bean counter for a couple days in the NKJV and started counting all the metaphors and repetitive words that start with "H." Then I categorized them. And wouldn't you know it, while working on some other patterns, I ran into a couple more. I also found changes in pattern style as John would change subject. Here is a little trivia question for you. How many times does John reference Jesus in 1st John? We've essentially read it in the last hour, so take a guess. More than fifty? More than a hundred? This is a list of metaphors that represent Jesus in 1st John: From the beginning 8, Word of life 1, Life 2, God is light 1, Truth (fellowship with Jesus) 6, Light 5, Word 2, Advocate 1, Propitiation 2, True light 1, Holy one 1, Word of God 1, Love of God 1, Son of God 7, Come in the flesh 2, Begotten Son 1, Savior of the world 1, Eternal life 3, and True 3 for a total of 49 metaphors.

I broke *He, His, Him* and *Himself* down to Jesus, the Father, the Christian Jew, and all others. Here is a snippet of what I found. The four *H*'s are used 169 times in the letter. 58 times for Christian Jews with 40 of those being the word *he*. 11 times for the Father with 9 of those being the word *His*. 17 for other that consist of Alexander, Cain and Paul. And 83 for Jesus, with 38 being the word *Him*. As I said already, *His Son* is always in the paragraph when the *H* word refers to the Father. This pattern becomes very helpful to understanding what John means. *His brother* is used 10 times and is a reference to Paul 9 times. The next pattern I noticed and tested amazed me, and seals the deal for what John truly wrote.

The word *Him* is used 51 times in 1st John. One time for Paul, one time for Cain and eleven times for Christian Jews. The other 38 times it is capitalized in the NKJV, and guess how many times the big *Him* is used for the Father? By using the instruction manual, written by John, the answer is zero. Thirty-eight times the big *Him* refers to Jesus Christ. Scholars will argue this point all day because scholars haven't read the Gospel, and the fact is every single big *Him* can be verified as Jesus by the Gospel of John. It's a big hint to what John was writing to the Christian Jews. In fact, it's more. It's the solution to what John is writing to the Christian Jews. Almost every metaphor that John uses to describe Jesus can be found in the first lines of the Gospel of John, including the big *Him*. I give partial quotes, "All things were made by him...In him was life...and the world was made by him, and the world knew him not...and his own received him not. But as many as received him...John bare witness of him." KJV. This *Him* is a description, or what I call a metaphor for Jesus, and the magic quilter is better than you ever knew. John is the magic man. Once you understand that every big *Him* is Jesus, you understand 1st John. I love my NKJV.

Jesus is referred to by name eleven times and referred to as God another forty-one times. That means in 1st John, Jesus is referenced 184 times or more.

When you know who Jesus is, and who the Father is, and who Paul and Alexander are in John's letter, then it makes total sense. Using a NKJV, before reading 1ˢᵗ John, take ten minutes and read John 13:31 through 18:38 and then John 1 to verse 15, and then read 1ˢᵗ John. You should start being able to see this. Metaphor free paraphrase.

1ˢᵗ John exposed

> That which was Jesus, which we have heard, which we have seen with our eyes, which we have looked upon, and our hands have handled, that is Jesus the Christ. Jesus was manifested, and we have seen, and bear witness, and declare to you that Jesus which was with the Father and was manifested to us; that which we have seen and heard we declare to you, that you also may have fellowship with us. And in truth our fellowship is with the Father and with His Son Jesus Christ. And these things we write to you that your joy may be full.

> This is the message that we have heard from Jesus and declare to you, that Jesus is Light and in Jesus is no darkness at all. If we say that we have fellowship with Jesus, and walk in the darkness, we lie and do not practice fellowship with Jesus. But if we walk in the Light as Jesus is in the Light, we have fellowship with one another, and the blood of Jesus Christ, God's Son cleanses us from all sin. If we say that we have no sin, we deceive ourselves, and the fellowship of Jesus is not in us. If we confess our sins, Jesus is faithful and just to forgive us our sins and to cleanse us from all unrighteousness. If we say that we have not sinned, we make Jesus a liar, and Jesus commandments are not in us. My church, these things I write to you, so you may not sin. And

if anyone sins, we have an Advocate with the Father, Jesus Christ the righteous. And Jesus Himself is the Propitiation for our sins, and not for ours only but for the whole world.

Now by this we know that we know Jesus, if we keep Jesus' commandments. He who says, "I know Jesus," and does not keep Jesus' commandments, is a liar, and the fellowship of Jesus is not in him. But whoever keeps Jesus' commandments, truly the love of Jesus is perfected in him. By this we know that we are in Jesus. He who says he abides in Jesus ought himself also to walk just as Jesus walked. Brethren, I write no new commandment to you, but an old commandment which you have had from Jesus. The old commandment is the commandment which you heard from Jesus. Again, this new commandment I write to you is true in Jesus and in you, because the darkness is passing away, and Jesus is already shining. He who says he is in Jesus, and hates Paul, is in sin until now. He who loves Paul abides in Jesus, and there is no cause for stumbling in him. But he who hates Paul is in sin and walks in sin, and does not know where he is going, because the sin has blinded his eyes.

I write to you, church, because your sins are forgiven you by Jesus' name's sake! I write to you, elders, because you have known Jesus, Jesus Christ! I write to you, new believers, because you have overcome the wicked one! I write to you, church, because you have known the Father! I have written to you, elders, because you have known Jesus, Jesus Christ! I have written to you, new believers, because you are strong, and the commandments of Jesus abide in you, and you have overcome the wicked one! Do not love the world or the things in the world. If anyone loves the world, the love of the Father is not in him. For all that is in the world; the lust of the flesh, the lust of the eyes, and the pride of life, is not of the Father but is of the world. And the world is passing away, and the lust of it; but he who does the will of Jesus abides forever. Church, it is the last hour; and as you have heard that the antichrist is coming, even now many antichrists have come, by which we know that it is the last hour. Alexander and his gang went out from us, but they were not of us; for if they had been of us, they would have continued with us; but they went out that they might be made manifest, that none of them were of us.

But you have an anointing from Jesus, and you know all things. I have not written to you because you do not know fellowship with Jesus, but because you know it, and that no lie is in this fellowship with Jesus. Who is a liar but he who denies that Jesus is the Christ? He is the antichrist who denies the Father and the Son. Whoever denies the Son does not have the Father either. He who acknowledges the Son has the Father also. Therefore, let that abide in you which you heard from Jesus. If what you heard from Jesus abides in you, you also will abide in the Son and in the Father. And this is the promise that Jesus has promised us; eternal life. These things I have written to you concerning Alexander and his gang who try to deceive you. But the anointing which you have received from Jesus abides in you, and you do not need that anyone teach you; but as the same anointing teaches you concerning all things, and is of Jesus, and is not a lie, and just as it has taught you, you will abide in Jesus. And now, church, abide in Jesus, that when Jesus appears, we may have confidence and not be ashamed before Jesus at Jesus' coming.

If you know that Jesus is righteous, you know that everyone who practices righteousness is born of Jesus. Behold what manner of love the Father has bestowed on us, that we should be called children of Jesus! Therefore, the world does not know us, because it did not know Jesus. Beloved, now we are the children of Jesus; and it has not yet been revealed what we shall be, but we know that when Jesus is revealed, we shall be like Jesus, for we shall see Jesus as Jesus is. And everyone who has this hope in Jesus purifies himself, just as Jesus is pure.

Whoever commits sin also commits lawlessness, and sin is lawlessness. And you know that Jesus was manifested to take away our sins, and in Jesus there is no sin. Whoever abides in Jesus does not sin. Whoever sins has neither seen Jesus nor known Jesus. Church, let no one deceive you. He who practices righteousness is righteous, just as Jesus is righteous. He who sins is of the devil, for the devil has sinned from the beginning. For this purpose, the Son of God was manifested, that Jesus might destroy the works of the devil. Whoever has been born of Jesus does not sin, for Jesus' seed remains in him; and he cannot sin, because he has been born of Jesus. In this the children of Jesus and the children of the devil are manifest: Whoever does not practice righteousness is not of Jesus, nor is he who does not love Paul. For this is the message that we heard from Jesus, that we should love one another, not as Cain who was of the wicked one and murdered his brother. And why did he murder him? Because his works were evil and his brother's righteous.

Do not marvel, my brethren, if the world hates you. We know that we have passed from death to life, because we love the brethren. He who does not love Paul abides in death. Whoever hates Paul is a murderer, and you know that no murderer has Jesus abiding in him. By this we know love, because Jesus laid down Jesus' life for us. And we also ought to lay down our lives for the brethren. But whoever has this world's goods, and sees his brother in need, and shuts up his heart from him, how does the love of Jesus abide in him? Church, let us not love in tongue, but in deed and in fellowship with Jesus. And by this we know that we are in fellowship with Jesus and shall assure our hearts before Jesus. For if our heart condemns us, Jesus is greater than our heart, and knows all things. Beloved, if our heart does not condemn us, we have confidence before Jesus. And whatever we ask we receive from Jesus, because we keep Jesus' commandments and do those things that are pleasing in Jesus sight. And this is Jesus commandment: that we should believe on the name of the Father's Son Jesus Christ and love one another, as Jesus gave us commandment. Now he who keeps Jesus' commandments abides in Jesus, and Jesus in him. And by this we know that Jesus abides in us, by the Spirit whom Jesus has given us.

Beloved, do not believe every spirit, but test the spirits to see whether they are of Jesus, because many false prophets have gone out into the world.

By this we know the Spirit of Jesus: Every spirit that confesses that Jesus Christ has come in the flesh is of Jesus, and every spirit that does not confess that Jesus Christ has come in the flesh is not of Jesus. And this is the antichrist, which you have heard was coming, and is now already in the world. You are of Jesus church, and have overcome Alexander and his gang, because Jesus who is in you is greater than Alexander who is in the world. Alexander and his gang are of the world. Therefore, they speak of the world, and the world hears them. We are of Jesus. He who knows Jesus hears us; he who is not of Jesus does not hear us. By this we know the spirit of fellowship with Jesus and the spirit of error.

Beloved, let us love one another, for love is of Jesus; and everyone who loves is born of Jesus and knows Jesus. He who does not love does not know Jesus, for Jesus is love. In this the love of the Father was manifested toward us, that the Father has sent the Father's only begotten Son into the world, that we might live through Jesus. In this is love, not that we loved the Father, but that the Father loved us and sent the His Son to be the propitiation for our sins. Beloved, if the Father so loved us, we also ought to love one another.

No one has seen the Father at any time, but if we love one another, Jesus abides in us, and Jesus' love has been perfected in us. By this we know that we abide in Jesus, and Jesus in us, because Jesus has given us Jesus' Spirit. And we have seen and testify that the Father has sent Jesus as the Savior of the World. Whoever confesses that Jesus is the Son of the Father, Jesus abides in him, and he in Jesus. And we have known and believed the love that Jesus has for us. Jesus is love, and he who abides in love abides in Jesus, and Jesus in him. Love has been perfected among us in this: that we may have boldness in the day of judgement; because as Jesus is, so are we in the world. There is no fear in love; but perfect love casts out fear, because fear involves torment. But he who fears has not been made perfect in love. We love Jesus because Jesus first loved us.

If someone says, "I love Jesus," and hates Paul, he is a liar; for he who does not love Paul whom he has seen, how can he love Jesus whom he has not seen? And this is the commandment we have from Jesus. That he who loves Jesus must love Paul also. Whoever believes that Jesus is the Christ is born of Jesus, and everyone who loves Jesus who was begot, also loves Paul who is begotten of Jesus.

By this we know that we love the children of Jesus, when we love Jesus and keep Jesus' commandments. For this is the love of Jesus; that we keep Jesus' commandments. And Jesus' commandments are not burdensome.

For whatever is born of Jesus overcomes the world. And this is the victory that has overcome the world; our faith. Who is he who overcomes the world, but he who believes that Jesus is the Son of the Father. This is Jesus who came by water and blood. Jesus Christ! Not only by water, but by water and blood. And it is the Spirit who bears witness, because the Spirit is fellowship with Jesus. For there are three that bear witness in heaven; the Father, Jesus, and the Holy Spirit; and these three are one. And there are three that bear witness on earth; the Spirit, the water, and the blood; and these three agree as one. If we receive the witness of men, the witness of the Holy Spirit is greater; for this is the witness of the Holy Spirit; that the Holy Spirit has testified of Jesus. He who believes in Jesus has the witness in himself; he who does not believe the Holy Spirit has made Jesus a liar, because he has not believed the testimony that the Holy Spirit has given of Jesus. And this is that testimony, that Jesus has given us eternal life. And this eternal life is through Jesus. He who has Jesus has eternal life and he who does not have Jesus does not have eternal life. These things I have written to you who believe in the name of the Jesus, that you may know that you have eternal life, and that you may continue to believe in the name of Jesus.

Now this is the confidence that we have in Jesus, that if we ask anything according to Jesus' will, Jesus hears us. And if we know that Jesus hears us, whatever we ask, we know that we have the petitions that we have asked of Jesus. If anyone sees his brother sinning a sin which does not lead to death, have him ask, and Jesus will give him eternal life, for those who commit sin not leading to death. There is sin leading to death. I do not say that he should pray about that. All unrighteousness is sin, and there is sin not leading to death.

We know that whoever is born of Jesus does not sin. But he who has been born of Jesus keeps himself, and the wicked one does not touch him. We know that we are of Jesus, and the whole world lies under the sway of the wicked one. And we know that Jesus has come and given us an understanding, that we may know Jesus who is true, and we are in Jesus who is true, in the Fathers Son Jesus Christ. This is the true God and eternal life.

Church, keep yourselves from idol makers. Amen.

This last line in this letter in all the Greek texts is the same, minus the amen in some, and this translated in Thayer's Lexicon under idols reads, "To guard oneself from all manner of fellowship with heathen worship." In other words, stay away from Alexander the coppersmith trinket maker and his gang.

The Gospel of John is a hologram inside the letter of 1ˢᵗ John. Every time you are not sure what something means, look in the hologram and the answer is right there.

I need to show the Deja Vue applied to 1ˢᵗ John, and I want to show the probabilities of John's patterns being an accident versus on purpose, and the connections in the writings as points of evidence to prove the letter is a reprimand, and further confirm the letter is against Alexander and for Paul, but this truck driver has reached his destination. It's time to stop and let it be what it is. I think, write it in dynamic translation, write it in modern, and then I have to say enough! If you're out there and still reading, then you either got the message, or you refuse to get the message and more instruction at this time is just overkill. It's time to finish. Most of this book has been written on scrap paper from work, on used route and weight sheets, that I make notes on the back of while I wait to get loaded or when I am forced to take a thirty-minute DOT break. I take those sheets and sort through them and make a chapter, and amazingly, it sort of makes sense when I'm done.

It's been seven weeks since I was talking about going to the big church that is preaching 1ˢᵗ John. My wife and I went to a different church that first week and it being Christmas time, the pastor preached a Grinch that stole Christmas thing. Then we snuck in the big church two weeks in a row, and the first time it was a Christmas message, and the second was a message about a cup of water. I watched some of the videos on line on 1st John from the big church and I just haven't been able to make myself sit through it live. I urgently want to finish this book and share it with anyone. I'm planning on starting with the pastor from the big church. I know my writing and style is second rate, and repetitious and ragged, but this whole thing has nothing to do with my writing. Lord let them see that this message is of You.

7

GO FISH

When they needed to pay the temple tax, Jesus told Peter to go to the water and drop in a line, and the first fish to bite, in its mouth will be a coin. Use that to pay the tax.

When the story of 1st John starts to come alive, you know that Paul has just been dragged out of the temple by an angry mob of Jews believing they are doing righteous service to God. And you can picture these young Christian Jews being easily convinced of Paul's crimes because of the false rumors that have been spread concerning him. And then for Alexander and the Jews from Asia to say that he brought a Gentile into the temple, well that's a pretty good reason to punish him. You can picture Paul in prison under Felix, for the crime of believing Jesus is God. And when you understand the story line you can see the reactions of the apostles, and you know this letter is a reprimand to those Christian Jews who days earlier were sure they were righteous.

When you know that your *brother* is Paul, and *they* are Alexander and his gang, and *Him* and the metaphors are Jesus, then you know that the story flops perfectly into the middle second half of the New Testament, and it all ties together. You can see that John writes a letter to Gaius of Philippi and has it delivered by Paul's traveling companions from there. And you can see that the church in 2nd John is one of the churches where Paul's traveling companions are from, and that John sent the letter by them. And not only do you see the connections in the New Testament present, but you can connect to the New Testament future, which is why Peter is in Rome and Silas is writing his letters. And it connects to almost every letter of Paul, and the whole New Testament is getting intertangled.

Remember the fishing net from the beginning. You can see your lures, the fish, the seaweed, the sand, the tangled lines. Your tackle box is a mess. The story of the New Testament that I'm sharing in 1st John is just like that, and real. And it's straight from the Bible. When you use the Bible as the reference for the story, you know who Paul is, and Alexander, and Jesus, and the Christian Jews of Jerusalem, and absolutely everything makes biblical sense. It is Bible correct and no scholar opinion is required to see the story. And that's the point I want to make here. You can see the story! You see who John is writing to and why. You know what the problem is and who the good guys and the bad guys are. They are people from the Bible. You know that the letter is a reprimand and a call to repentance and fellowship. Just like investigative reporting, you know the who, what, when, where, and why!

In the story that the scholars tell, you don't know who the letter is written to or where it's written. Your told it's about love, but it is contradicting to itself and to the Gospel. Why would John write a letter that says love one another, and I write a new commandment to love your brother, if it's the same thing? Why would he write love one another and follow God's commands if they were already doing it? There is no legitimate *what* to the scholars' letter! And the when and why are to fight fictitious Gnostics created by the Tooth Fairy like enemy, the mighty Cerinthus? Seriously, who is Cerinthus? There is no evidence. Remember my pretend murder story and how ridicules it was that the 2nd guy was accused on small circumstantial evidence. Well, that evidence equals a mountain compared to the evidence against Cerinthus. But it doesn't matter as long as you're not attacking the real enemy.

In chapter one, I said, the thread that ties the books of the New Testament together is like that ball of tangled fishing line in your fishing net. That giant mess inside the net is the New Testament. The twenty-seven lures represent the twenty-seven books, and the tackle box is the book cover, and all that messy line is the leaders attached to those lures, and they belong to you. When you left your house, they were all in their proper compartments, ready to use, but stored neatly out of the way, and then somehow while netting this fish, you knocked the whole open tackle box into the net when you reached for your pliers. What a mess! So what would you do? Let me give you some choices. Fisherman A retrieves the pliers and removes the hook from the lip of the fish and lets it go. He carefully and patiently untangles each line and this time ties the leader neatly so that no way it can tangle again. Then he stores each lure in its designated compartment. He closes the lid on the box and fastens a clasp so that there's no way it can come open on accident. He takes the box home and stores it on a shelf in the garage and probably never uses it again. Fisherman B takes the fish home and eats it. He dumps all the lures and line right back into the box after shaking off the sand and pulling out the seaweed. He just stuffs it in there and makes sure he has it all and shuts the lid. Fisherman C is so distraught at how big of a mess catching one fish can be, that he walks the net over to a dumpster and tosses the whole thing, fish and all. Which one are you, A, B or C? It depends? Do you know it's a parable? If the lures represent the New Testament, and the leaders on those lures are the connection between the Books, why would you unravel them and separate the Books? Why would you store them or toss them? If the lures represent the New Testament and the tackle box is the cover, what does the sand represent? It's my parable, I'll tell you. The sand represents the worldly influence on the Word, and the seaweed making the mess look worse than it is, is the sway of the evil one. And the fish is the Bread of Life. Now that you know the answers to the metaphors, is your answer a little easier? As for me, I'm eating that symbolic fish! What is fruit?

My goal in showing Paul in 1st John with the four discernments from my little letter was to give you New Testament knowledge. I hope that you received what I was trying to share. Besides just telling you who your brother is, I made a grand attempt to show you how to find him by using tools other than what the scholars are selling. An ancient Chinese proverb says, "Catch a man a fish, you feed him for a day. Teach a man to fish, and you feed him for life." That ancient Chinese proverb makes sense. I showed you what 1st, 2nd, and 3rd John say, and as I was doing it, I was still learning myself. Did I get everything? No. Did I get it one hundred percent right? I bet not. But just like St. Irenaeus, I know that what I shared is not insufficient in the brain. I actually had to stop looking because every day the Word was giving me more. During the venture of this book, I have had to purposely not read half the New Testament because I already had sufficient evidence and was over the limit I could manage. I can't wait to finish these few last pages of this book so I can open some other books and see how they tie in.

The ties I've shown in the New Testament are just the beginning of what is there. I just shared what shows your *brother*. Using the same discernments and finding some more of your own, you will discover Gospel truths in the New Testament that you've never seen before. Look past the chapters and verses, and read the letters. Look for clues in the letter as to the who, what, when, where and why. There is always something there. Look for the connections to the other letters. Remember the letter was written in ancient Greek and translated several times before modern English, and even though we have excellent copies of the Greek text to compare, the translation is sometimes hard to understand because of metaphors and other practices we are not familiar with. Yet, it's always going to be in line with the Gospels which makes figuring it out fun. Yep, I just clumped challenging, frustrating, irritating, and satisfying in to the word fun. After reading this little book, metaphors, and clues, and connections in the New Testament are going to jump at you from everywhere.

Despite my resentment to scholars on 1st John, they usually have the translation correct. They just have no clue to the time line or story line and that's just what scholars always share in the study Bible right before the letters, so just skip that. Read the Gospel or letter and make your own assessments. When you find some new thing you never knew before, test it, and expect at least half the time to be wrong. I'll give an example.

I know that the Gospel of John was written before the Epistles of John, that were written right after the return of Paul from his third missionary journey and then tossed from the temple. I have plenty of evidence from the Bible to prove that. Furthermore, the contradicting evidence that scholars use which comes from St Irenaeus, I have shown in this little book, and it is easy to assess that the Biblical evidence is correct. The Bible trumps hearsay. My focus now as I read the letters of the New Testament is to look for clues that will tell me how long the Gospel of John has been on the scene as a Gospel and distributed. When Paul comes back from his third missionary journey with Luke and his other companions, they meet first with the apostles. Luke is a companion of the apostles. They're old friends, and everybody is sharing. While Paul is in the temple being cleansed, I see Luke spending his days making a copy of John's Gospel, as it was a thing at this time. But then I think, what if Luke got the Gospel from John at the return of the first missionary journey? It's possible, and I'm still working on this theory. Is it true? I don't know, but as I read I keep sniffing for clues. I thought once

I had the proof in the pudding, but testing it, I was wrong. At the end of John's instruction manual, Pilate says, "What is truth?" And when Paul wrote his first letter to Timothy, which is before the end of the third missionary journey, he writes that Jesus gave the good confession before Pontius Pilate. I thought I had something. I thought, Paul read John's Gospel and knew this. That is wrong. Paul easily could have read Matthew or Mark's Gospel and knew this, or even been told by Luke or others. I still will be constantly looking for clues for the earlier date of John's Gospel. Is it important? No. Is it interesting and challenging? Yes. I guess my point here is, to have fun with this new knowledge, but don't make the Bible say something that it doesn't, because that's already been done. When you get it right, you'll know it, because it fits all the Gospels, and the rest of the Bible including the Old Testament.

This is my present time line for the Books of the New Testament: First Matthew, then Mark and then John, Romans, 1st Corinthians, 1st Thessalonians and 1st Timothy, then maybe Luke, then 1st, 2nd and 3rd John, followed by the rest of Paul's Epistles, and then Peter's Epistles, then Acts, James, Jude, and then Revelation. I said this is my present timeline, because it could change. There is biblical evidence and worldly evidence and a story line, and the more I read, the more I learn. There are clues and proofs in the New Testament stories that are evidence for this order, and that in itself is another book of investigative information. So instead of me feeding you, I just have to say it, "Go fish!" You think the patterns I showed in 1st John were all there is? Wait till you compare the Gospels.

When truth is exposed and verified it will usually win the day. These four discernments together become a solid verifiable evidence that cannot be denied. Any one of these discernments by itself can easily be countered and denied by falsehoods from the other three discernments. As I started seeing the truth, I would attempt to explain one simple discernment at a time, always to end up as though I were babbling of endless genealogies. If I were to say, John is writing about his brother Paul, I am told that the onslaught of evidence from the early church and scholars prove beyond any doubt, that John wrote his letters in the nineties to combat Gnosticism. I am told I have an interesting theory, but it has no foundation and this is why those empowered with the work of God must first be educated in the fundamental truths. See, I'm just a truck driver and all I have is my NKJV without the pertinent study information, so I concede that there are things that I don't know. Three months later, after a study of 2nd and 3rd John, I say, "Hey, look, 3rd John is proof that John wrote his Books in the fifties," and over coffee I show good evidence. I am told I make good points, but I should think of applying to seminary for some proper training, because it is obvious from the evidence in the Bible, it says that John is battling Gnosticism. I'm still looking for this evidence.

This makes me crazy. The hardest part is the apathy. We are at church to learn and come closer to Jesus Christ, and whatever we are doing at church this week is the most important thing in the whole world, and the least important is, (at least it seems that way to me) is the Word of God.

This little book is based on one foundation. The Word of God. I believe the Holy Bible to be the true Word of God. That is the whole foundation. I'm just a truck driver with a high school education, that lives in a recreation vehicle, in a trailer park, but Jesus has allowed me to write this book because I have passion for His Word. I seek Him, and the truth in Him. This book is not a reprimand. This book is an awakening. It's time to get out your tackle box and tie on some leaders to a couple lures and toss a line in the water. Jesus Christ is the Son of God in whom I abide.

Two thousand years ago Jesus walked the earth and was eighteen years old, and five hundred years ago Erasmus made a complete New Testament in the Greek for the masses, and Luther took that and freed religion. Jesus said, "Destroy this temple, and in three days I will rise it up." and in 2nd Peter, Peter said, "But, beloved, be not ignorant of this one thing, that one day is with the Lord as a thousand years, and a thousand years as one day." And in Revelation, John writes, "And they lived and reigned with Christ a thousand years.", with those who died for His name's sake, and "This is the first resurrection." The Gospel is waking, and Jesus is coming and apathy is His enemy.

What is fruit? For me, fruit is truth in Jesus Christ. And what is truth? For me, truth is fellowship with Jesus Christ. So, what is fruit? It is Him in whom I abide. Eat your fruit.

KJV APPENDIX

Chapter 2

Acts 17:23 For I passed by
John 1:1-3 In the beginning was
John 1:1 partial; In the beginning was
John 1:3 partial; All things were made
John 1:4 partial; In him was life
John 1:5 partial; and the darkness
1st Tim 6:20-21 partial; O Timothy
1st Tim Paraphrased
Acts 8:24 Then answered Simon

Chapter 3

3rd John complete

Chapter 4

Mark 4:3-20 Hearken; behold
Luke 8:10-15 And he said, unto
Matt 13:10-12 And the disciples came
Matt 13:13-17 Therefore speak I
1st Peter 1:1-2 partial; To the strangers
1st Peter 5:13 The church that is at
2nd John complete
3rd John 1:3 For I rejoiced greatly
1st John 1:1 That which was from

1st Peter 5:13 partial; The church that is at

John 6:35 I am the bread

John 8:12 partial; I am the light

John 10:19 I am the door

John 10:14 I am the good shepherd

John 11:25 partial; I am the resurrection

John 14:16 partial; I am the way

John 15:5 I am the vine

Genesis 1:1-3 In the beginning

John 1:1-4 In the beginning

1st John 1:1-3 That which was from

2nd John 1:1-2 The elder unto the elect

1st John 1:1-3 partial; and truly our fellowship

1st John 1:1-6 If we say that we have

1st John 2:4-5 partial; He that saith, I know

1st John 2:21 I have not written unto you

1st John 2:27 But the anointing which ye

1st John 4:6 We are of God:

1st John 5:20 And we know that the Son

2nd John 1:7 For many deceivers are entered

John 1:14 And the Word was made flesh

1st John 2:22-23 Who is a liar but he

1st John 4:2-3 partial; Hereby ye know the spirit

John 6:53 Verily, Verily, I say unto you

John 6:32 partial; I am the bread of life

2nd John 1:10 partial; If there come any unto

1st Cor 15:29-34 Else what shall they do

1st Cor 15:3-4 For I delivered unto you

1st Cor 15:12 Now if Christ be preached

1st Cor 15:32 partial; let us eat and drink

2nd Cor 12:19 My grace is sufficient

Chapter 5

2nd John 1:8 Look to yourselves
1st John 2:27-28 But the anointing
1st Thess 5:21 prove all things
John 13:34-35 A new commandment
John 15:12 This is my commandment
John 15:17 These things I command you
1st John 3:11 For this is the message
1st John 3:23 And this is his commandment
1st John 4:7 Beloved, let us love
1st John 4:11 Beloved, if God so loved
John 16:1-4 partial; These things I have spoken
1st John 2:9-10 He that saith he is
1st John 3:10 In this the children
1st John 3:14 partial; We know that we
1st John 4:20-5:1 If a man say
1st John 2:13 partial; I write unto you little
1st John 2:13 partial; I have written unto you fathers
1st John 2:14 partial; I have written unto you fathers
1st John 2:19 They went out from us
1st John 2:24 Let that therefore abide
1st John 3:11 For this is the message that ye
Matt 3:17 This is my beloved Son
Mark 9:7 This is my beloved Son
John 1:1 In the beginning was the Word
1st John 2:7-8 Brethren, I write no new
1st John 3:23 And this is his commandment
1st John 4:21-5:1 And this commandment have we
1st John 5:1 Whosoever believeth that
1st John 4:20 If a man say, I love God
John 17:22-23 And the glory which thou

Chapter 6

1st John 5:1 Whosoever believeth that
1st John 2:7 Brethren, I write no new
1st John 2:6 He that saith he
1st John 5:1 Whosoever believeth that
John 1:1 partial; In the beginning was
John 1:2 partial; The same was in the
1st John 1:1 partial; That which was from
John 1:4 In him was life
John 1:9 That was the true light
John 1:14 partial; of the only begotten
John 14:6 partial; I am the way
John 18:37 partial; Everyone that is of the
1st John 1:3 partial; truly our fellowship
John 18:38 partial; What is truth
John 1:14 And the word was made
1st John 4:2 partial; Every spirit that confesseth
John 5:8 partial; Rise, take up thy bed
John 5:16-18 And therefore did the Jews
John 8:58 Verily, Verily, I say unto
John 8:59 Then took they up stones
John 9:1 And as Jesus passed by
John 10:24 partial; If thou be the Christ
John 10:25 partial; I told you and ye
John 10:30 I and my father are one
John 11:53 Then from that day forth
John 13:34 A new commandment I give
John 14:15 If ye love me, keep
John 14:21 He that hath my commandments
John 14:23 If a man love me, he will keep
John 15:10 If ye keep my commandments
John 15:12 This is my commandment
John 15:17 These things I command you
1st John 2:13 partial; I write unto you fathers

1st John 2:12 partial; I write unto you, little
1st Cor 15:32 partial; If after the manner of men
1st John 2:18 partial; Even now are there many
1st John 2:19 partial; they went out from us
1st John 4:4 partial; because greater is he that
1st John 4:5 partial; They are of the world
1st John 5:21 partial; Little children, keep
1st John 1:3 partial; truly our fellowship
Luke 22:70 partial; Art thou then the Son
Luke 22:70 partial; Ye say that I am
John 1:3 partial; All things were made
John 1:4 partial; In him was life
John 1:10 partial; and the world was made
John 1:11 partial; and his own received him not
John 1:12 partial; But as many as received
John 1:15 partial; John bare witness of

Chapter 7

John 18:38 partial; what is truth
John 2:19 partial; Destroy this temple
2nd Peter 3:8 But, beloved, be not ignorant
Rev 20:4 And they lived and reigned
Rev 20:5 This is the first resurrection

E
G
I
R

Who is your brother in 1st john, on the web.